SOCCER COACHING
AND
TEAM MANAGEMENT

SOCCER
COACHING
AND
TEAM MANAGEMENT

BY
MALCOLM COOK

FOREWORD BY
LAWRIE McMENEMY

EP PUBLISHING LIMITED

Published by EP Publishing Limited
© **Malcolm Cook 1982**

ISBN 0 7158 0833 8 (cased)
     0 7158 0795 1 (limp)

Phototypesetting by CTL Computer Typesetters Ltd, Leeds

Printed and bound in England by Camelot Press, Southampton

Acknowledgements

The author and publishers would like to thank the following
for kind permission to reproduce copyright material:

All Sport: pp. 29, 36, 43, 81, 88, 104, 115
Syndication International: pp. 76, 80, 95, 120, 125
Football Association: p. 19
Weekly News: p. 23
Telegraph & Argus: p. 106

Special thanks are due to the following people and
organisations, without whose generous advice and assistance
this book would never have seen the light of day:

Bradford University soccer team
Mick Bullock, Team Manager, Halifax Town F.C.
Allen Wade, Director of Coaching to the Football Association
Charles Hughes, Assistant Director of Coaching to the
Football Association
Norman Hunter, Team Manager, Barnsley F.C.
Gordon Jago, Executive Vice President/Head Coach,
Tampa Bay Rowdies F.C.
Bobby Moore, ex-England Captain, Sports Executive
George Mulhall, ex-Team Manager, Bolton Wanderers F.C.
Lawrie McMenemy, Team Manager, Southamptom F.C.
Roy McFarland, Team Manager and Mick Jones,
Coach, Bradford City F.C.
Jock Stein, Team Manager, Scotland International team
Dr Maurice Yaffe, Psychological Consultant to Crystal
Palace F.C.
Mitre Sports Ltd
Patrick (UK) Ltd
Rollalong Ltd
Swintex Ltd

FOREWORD

My experience in soccer, ranging from schoolboy teams to the top professionals, has led me to believe that although there are varying degrees of emphasis, commitment and sophistication in soccer coaching and team management, basically the same major factors are relevant at all levels.

Malcolm Cook, a fully qualified Football Association coach, has made a detailed study over a number of years in the professional game of the key factors which contribute to successful coaching and team management. He has consulted many of the leading soccer authorities for advice, and confirmation on his views of the psychological pressures which inevitably affect the coach or team manager. This latter area is as yet largely unexplored territory and there is scant educational instruction or information readily available. The book is concerned with vital elements such as team spirit, communication, match analysis, motivation, club organisation, soccer skill learning plus, of course, coaching and team management with appropriate guidelines for the individual to consider when dealing with his own team.

Coaching and team management are not just about practice sessions, team selection and passing on technical and tactical information to players. 'Man-management' is as important as knowledge of the game, for no matter how much the team manager or coach knows, or thinks he knows, if he cannot convey his ideas effectively then he will surely struggle. Some tend to be very stereotyped and inflexible in their approach to the team members, seeking almost total conformity from them, which in certain circumstances creates conflict, especially with the so-called 'problem' players. In general, a coach's, and team manager's ability to handle his players improves with experience. I have found that a team manager usually benefits from having been a coach first. He will be more sympathetic with his club's coach and will want to work in harmony with him to create that valuable partnership which is essential for success. Some people seem able to combine the dual roles of coach and team manager, but the majority work either as one or the other, each forming an integral part of the staff team. The information contained in this book will help both to avoid repeating previous mistakes and to recognise new problems as they arise. It should cultivate a more positive approach to everyday dealings with the many personalities in the soccer game.

All aspiring coaches and team managers, whether at schoolboy, youth, senior or professional level, require advice and guidance in these demanding occupations. At the moment there is little scope for the more experienced to pass on relevant information to their inexperienced colleagues who may be embarking on what is all too often a short career where many flounder without the correct preparation for the job. This book, which is long overdue, will prove to be a most valuable aid and reference source to soccer coaches and team managers at every level of the game and it will especially help those starting out for the first time. I have been greatly impressed by the author's all-round knowledge, presentation and attention to detail. I only wish *Soccer Coaching and Team Management* had been available when I set out on my soccer career.

CONTENTS

INTRODUCTION

Soccer coaching and team management is a multi-faceted occupation. It involves the effective communication of technical knowledge, important decision making, and the delicate handling of many different sorts of temperaments, as well as the ability to demonstrate in practice a high standard of soccer. This book stems largely from my own experiences as player, teacher, coach and team manager, but I have also drawn from those of several well-known colleagues in the profession. My main aims have been to discuss the application of theory on the field; to set down major areas of concern; and to suggest guidelines for consideration by any aspiring manager or coach. The book does not attempt to give cut-and-dried answers; the problems vary too much from club to club to allow for that.

The game of soccer has taken dramatic strides forward over the last few decades in the areas of physical fitness, tactics and technical skill. However, with the modern team being so much more organised and efficient, particularly defensively, it is not always easy to see these improvements since the players have less time in which to display their talents. Today's teams have to work much harder and cover far greater distances than their predecessors, and coaches and managers require a deeper understanding of the key factors which make for tactical development. Many have made concentrated studies of principles and systems of team play, strategy, and general soccer skills. The coach's ability to encourage both individual players and the team as a whole has come from observing others at work, through trial and error, from discussion with colleagues, and, of course, from his own past experiences as a player. It is clear that any manager, or coach, can only help players achieve their potential if he has the necessary knowledge and expertise in all areas of the sport. This must include an understanding of physical conditioning, motivation, and even basic psychology. Competent organisation, therefore, together with greater flexibility among players, has resulted in a narrowing of the gap between the top professionals and the lower league and non-league clubs.

Much progress has also been made with equipment; for example, lightweight boots and footballs allow players a more sensitive 'touch' with the ball. Artificial pitches are now available, plus a large amount of training equipment which is geared to aid coach and players.

I have spent many years compiling this book, gradually adding notes taken from my observations and experiences of difficult soccer problems. I now feel I have reached a number of conclusions about players' and teams' individual needs, and how they can best be helped to fulfil their ambitions. I hope this book will set these out in an easily accessible form, catering for both the psychological and organisational sides to soccer coaching and team management.

CLUB ORGANISATION

Duties and responsibilities

In any club involving people, decisions and jobs to be done, the team manager, no matter to whom he delegates, must in the final analysis take the responsibility. For this reason he must see that particular attention is paid to detail and that the club is efficiently organised and well run. Good organisation ensures that time and effort are not wasted and that the staff know their duties and responsibilities. The club should aim to be a smooth running machine with everything geared to success, especially prior to a competitive match when players are tense and emotionally involved. Poor organisation can show in a variety of ways, from practice balls not being properly inflated to the team arriving late for a match. Errors can occur at any level because of lack of forethought. For example, in the World Cup Finals in Argentina in 1978, the French team made the unfortunate error of bringing shirts too similar in colour to those of their opponents and the match was delayed for about 30

11

minutes while members of their staff attempted to borrow an unfamiliar green and white strip. The team manager is there to see that errors are of a minor nature and infrequent. There are four steps that the team manager can take to ensure that everyone knows his duties and responsibilities, keeping in mind that the functions of the team manager vary from club to club and at different levels of the game.

★ Staff meetings
★ Delegation of responsibilities
★ Flow charts
★ Check-lists

Staff meetings

Staff meetings should be initiated to discuss the running of the club. The team manager should listen to suggestions and give staff a chance to air their views; after he has collected all the data he must decide who is best suited to which job and inform each person individually of this. The team manager should not hold many staff meetings, otherwise they will lose their impact.

Delegation

When he has decided on the best person for each job he must delegate accordingly, making sure that a task is not beyond each person's capabilities. No one should be just left to do the job – the team manager should ask him or her to report on progress every so often and must be prepared to modify the job or change the person if necessary. Therefore, the more responsible staff should be delegated to the more responsible jobs. The delegation of jobs to appropriate people is one of the major roles of the team manager.

Flow chart

The flow chart is a simple idea but makes an effective contribution to clarity of organisation by showing visually, to all staff concerned, how the different units of the club operate and who is responsible to whom. A typical flow chart is given here, showing the different job responsibilities of each staff member. The flow chart illustrates the structure of a professional league club's youth scheme, and originates from when I was the Youth Development Manager to that club.

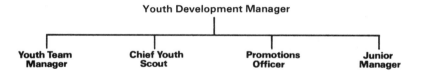

Roles & Responsibilities

RESPONSIBILITIES

YOUTH DEVELOPMENT MANAGER

Function: The supremo of the scheme, with responsibility for implementing the club's youth policy.
(1) To co-ordinate with the first team manager to implement club policy.
(2) To liaise with the reserve team manager to effect the promotion of youth players into that team when they are ready.
(3) To work with the youth staff and to plan ahead, motivate staff, organise the available resources to maximum effect and generally provide the necessary 'back-up' for all sections.

YOUTH TEAM MANAGER

Function: Responsible for the youth team.
(1) To coach, train and prepare the youth team.
(2) To select the youth team.
(3) To communicate with the youth players about matches and the training and coaching programme.

CHIEF YOUTH SCOUT

Function: The recruitment of promising young players.
(1) To implement a local scouting network plus hiring of scouts.
(2) To organise regular trial matches for recommended young players in the 14–17 age range.
(3) To have sole responsibility for signing associate schoolboy players.

PROMOTIONS OFFICER

Function: The positive promotion of the youth scheme plus the formation of a limited scheme to raise cash for the youth scheme.
(1) To act as public relations officer for the youth scheme and to obtain regular positive publicity via the local media.
(2) To set up sponsorship and other limited money-raising schemes to gain materials and cash for the youth scheme's development.

JUNIOR MANAGER

Function: The development of interest in the younger age range.
(1) To promote and organise coaching clinics for junior players and a junior boys supporters' club.
(2) To assist the youth team manager and chief youth scout when required and available.
(3) To set up a 'ball-boy' scheme for first team matches.

Check-list

Each staff member should draw up a check-list to serve as a memory aid and to ensure that nothing is left to chance. Where the flow chart shows his responsibilities in general terms, the check-list is more detailed and specific. The check-list should be simple, easy to read and put in a prominent place so that the person concerned can go over the items when the time comes to do so. The sample check-list is for the planning of matches. However, the organisational requirements will vary from club to club.

MATCH CHECK-LIST

HOME:
(1) Contact opponents.
(2) Contact referee and linesmen.
(3) Contact players and staff.
(4) Facilities
    (a) clean dressing rooms and baths.
    (b) lay out playing kit and towels.
    (c) lay out practice balls and equipment.
    (d) lay out medical box.

AWAY:
(1) Transport to venue
    (a) mode of travel.
    (b) insurance and cost.
    (c) meeting arrangements.
(2) Playing kit.
(3) Accommodation – lunch or overnight hotel stays should be scheduled in advance.

A standard club letter could be sent to the opponents, referee and linesmen, players and staff, with a tear-off section to be returned to the club to confirm their availability. The following details should be enclosed in the letter:

★ the date, day and match kick-off time
★ a map showing the route to the ground
★ the colours of the home club
★ any other relevant information

The check-list ensures a systematic procedure which should make the staff members' organisation easier and more efficient.

Areas for organisation

The match

The basic organisation and administration for the match should be carried out by the appropriate staff who have been allocated these tasks by the team manager. The club should have a special team selection sheet which is put up on a noticeboard. The sample team selection sheet (see below) could be duplicated with spaces for the team manager to record each player's individual performance and the general team performance, the result, scorers, conditions, and also the team manager's performance rating for each player. The sheet can be folded over so that only the team selection sheet is displayed to the players. When the match is finished, the team manager can remove the form from the notice-board and file his match details for future reference.

Savile F.C.
Team Performance Report Sheet:

Result: _____ Scorers: _____

General Conditions: _____

Team	Individual Performance:		R
	1		
	2		
	3		
	4		
	5		
	6		
	7		
	8		
	9		
	10		
	11		
	12		

Team Performance: _____

Savile F.C.
Team Selection Sheet:

Match: _____ v. _____

Venue: _____ Date: _____ K.O: _____

Team:

	1	
	2	Reserves to attend:
	3	_____
	4	Meet: _____
	5	
	6	Time: _____
	7	Additional information:
	8	
	9	
	10	
	11	
	12	

Sub: _____ Signed: _____

The training and coaching programme

This should be planned jointly between the team manager and the coach who should consult one another to ensure that they are both working along similar lines. If the team manager is not a coach, he must leave the more specific details to the coach, who will be more actively involved with the players in the squad. The programme will be concerned with four major areas:

★ Technical skill
★ Tactical play
★ Physical fitness
★ Pressure conditioning

TECHNICAL SKILL

The programme will be aimed at improving the reliability of each player's existing technical skills and extending the range of his repertoire by introducing him to new technical skills. The problem here is that time

15

and patience are required by the coach and player before new technical skills are fully learned, and some team managers believe that they do not have the time to wait until the technical development of the player comes to fruition. It is vitally important that younger players learn and practise more and new technical skills while older players need to practise and rehearse the basic technical skills to ensure success. If the coach does not have much practice time to spend with his players, he should concentrate on the technical skills that will guarantee his players and team the greatest degree of success.

★ Shooting:
this is most important, as scoring goals is essentially what the game is all about, and it should be practised at every session wherever possible.
★ Passing:
the game is also a passing game and the team which passes the ball more accurately to maintain possession, often controls the game more easily and plays with greater efficiency, style and confidence.
★ Crossing and heading:
an enormous number of goals, at all levels of the game, originate from flank crosses, which often put defensive players at a disadvantage, as they find it much more difficult to observe the ball and their immediate attacker once the ball is transferred to a wide position. Defenders and attackers require regular practice in dealing with high and low crosses.

Special provision needs to be made for the goalkeepers in the squad in order to develop or maintain their level of technical skill. Often, the goalkeeper does not receive the type or intensity of work that he requires, and as a result he loses confidence in his technical ability. The goalkeeper is probably the most important member of the team for often it is literally in his hands whether the match is won or lost! He needs regular and realistic practice of such aspects as shot-stopping, positioning, kicking and taking crosses.

The technical skill work throughout the season should be geared to the competitive match by the intelligent application of unopposed and opposed practices and other 'pressures' at the appropriate stages of the players' development.

TACTICAL PLAY

In terms of time, difficulty and importance for the team manager and coach, emphasis should be given to the development of tactical play. It is often very difficult to get players to co-ordinate effectively as a team instead of as eleven individuals. The tactical knowledge of each player in the team will determine how far the coach can go with tactics. The programme should be concerned with developing to the maximum potential each player's tactical understanding and his role and responsibilities in the team's general system of play. Tactical play and restarts, such as free-kicks and corner kicks, need to be discussed, rehearsed and practised often in small groups, larger groups and then in a full eleven versus eleven game. The team manager and coach would do well to remember the tactical factors which bring success and ensure that these factors are practised continually and generally brought to the players' notice in a positive fashion. With this in mind, it is vital that the team practises and rehearses restarts, both defensively and in attack, as it is known that a large number of goals scored at all levels of the game come from corner-kicks or other restarts.

PHYSICAL FITNESS

Fairly often, when joining a new club, coaches immediately increase the training workload of the players. This is probably intended to make the team fitter so that they can cover more ground and generally become harder to beat. However, it can also be a psychological aid in that players can generally become fit in a shorter period of time than it takes the coach to develop technical skill or tactical play. The fitness programme for the squad needs to cater for individual work and weaknesses, as well as work of a general nature. This will often be very difficult, especially when there is little training time or a lack of facilities and equipment. However, if one player has a major weakness, it is a threat to the team and as such must be given specific attention somewhere in the programme. For example, a player may be a good performer when in possession of the ball but lack speed to get away from close-marking defenders. Another player may play well as a full back for three quarters of the match but go to pieces in the final quarter through lack of strength and endurance. The major fitness factor which needs to be developed to a reasonable level in soccer is the quality of endurance for ninety minutes, or two hours when extra time is played. The running is broken up with flat-out sprints over various distances, and slower running over much longer distances. The coach must calculate the average distance which players cover in the competitive match and develop their capacity to withstand this workload in training sessions.

PRESSURE CONDITIONING

The programme should set out to build up team spirit as a policy by planning social events where the players have opportunities to mix together. Within its coaching and training plan, the programme should seek to encourage the proper levels of aggression, determination and self-control. The coach can, by the sensible introduction of stress, teach players to play to the maximum in the competitive game. Players who always play in nicely controlled practice situations, where the mood, though workmanlike, is lacking in realism, will often find it very difficult to cope in the heat of a competitive match when the tackles are flying in and emotions are high. The coach can introduce 'stress' or 'pressure' in practice games or competitions, by 'conditioning games' where players need to do things much quicker, as in 'one-touch' soccer where each player has only one touch of the ball. When players or teams are unsuccessful, they can be given as a forfeit practice shuttle runs or increased physical work. Often the coach, by his attitude can make the situation more tense and thus increase the practice mood and tempo. Obviously there is the danger of confrontation between players but provided the coach and the players realise that they need to learn, practise and rehearse to keep their technical skills, ability and emotions in check, then it is extremely advantageous to increase the practice tempo. The programme must also make a positive attempt to cater for players who find it difficult to integrate socially with other team members.

The team manager and coach, when deciding on the order of priorities of the coaching and training programme, must consider the following factors:

Time:
The number and length of the practice sessions.
Area:
What area is available? Indoor or outdoor? A training pitch?
Daylight:
In winter, daylight limits time on a pitch unless floodlights are available.
Staff:
The number, ability and availability of assistant coaches and staff is an important consideration.
Equipment:
The availability of portable goals, the number of practice footballs and training bibs.

SEASONAL VARIATIONS

When planning the coaching and training programme for the season, the team manager and coach must take the three separate but inter-related phases of the season into consideration.

THE CLOSE SEASON

Physically and psychologically, the player needs a break at the end of the playing season so that he can recharge his batteries for the next season. It is important that he maintains his general fitness by engaging in other sports or leisure pursuits and that he does not overeat. The team manager can set weight and/or fitness targets for when the player reports back for training to his club. In fact, some professional clubs impose fines on players who fail to get under the target bodyweight. There is not a lot that the team manager can do in advance, though, as much will depend on the player's lifestyle.

PRE-SEASON

This is the period between first reporting back for training and playing the first competitive match. The objective during this phase is to take the players from a basic fitness, technical skill, tactical and psychological level through to peak preparation for the competitive match. The work will be of a gradual nature which gets increasingly more intense.

There is a lot to be done during this phase to bring players to the peak required in the limited time available before the first match. As mentioned earlier, it is a big help to the coach if the players report back for pre-season training with a reasonable level of physical fitness, so that the conditioning work starts at a higher level and the workload for the players is not so severe. Some soccer clubs leave their training grounds or areas open one or two evenings a week during the close season for voluntary training. Whatever the method, a basic level of physical fitness must be reached during the pre-season period. The coach will also spend much time on developing the team's tactical pattern, restart rehearsal, technical skill development and generally sharpening up the players for the battles to come. The team manager will be involved in team formations and how certain players are adjusting to the roles asked of them. For this reason, the team manager should arrange pre-season practice matches against suitable opposition.

THE COMPETITIVE SEASON

When the competitive season begins, there is increased physical and psychological pressure on the team to win. The team manager and coach must try to develop a regular training and coaching pattern of work which varies in intensity according to the timing of the competitive matches, ensuring that the players are at their peak physically and psychologically for the match. It is not easy to maintain this training rhythm because of such factors as cancelled matches and training sessions, or players unavailable because of injury or work. Whatever the problems, the coach must try to develop a training routine to which the players get accustomed and from which they benefit. The competitive phase is the most important one for the team manager and coach, so good planning, organisation and administration of the programme are vital.

Part of an F.A. Year Planner.

TRAINING AND COACHING DIARY

The coach should keep a diary of the team's training and coaching work so that he can assess and monitor the effect of the work on his players. Liverpool F.C. is well-known for its training diary where full details of everything connected with preparation is recorded. The general objectives should be entered in the diary and a more detailed plan should be transferred to the coach's schedule sheet for the session. In the coaching section, items such as technical skills, tactical and team play, restart rehearsal and goalkeeping should be entered, while in the training section, items such as endurance, speed and power should be included. All matches should be entered with comments on each session. The following is a sample page from a training and coaching diary.

Daily Record

January 1983 _____ Phase: _____

Week No: _____

Day	Date	Coaching	Training
Mon	2nd		
Tue	3rd		
Wed	4th		
Thu	5th		
Fri	6th		
Sat	7th		

General club administration

The team manager and the coach can save time and effort by ensuring that as much information as possible on staff, players and general club matters is recorded and readily available. There is nothing more frustrating than trying to get hold of someone when you do not know their address or telephone number, or the relevant information for some club problem not being available. There is no reason why the training and coaching diary cannot include sections to help the team manager and coach to organise, administrate and communicate more effectively. For example:

★ Squad information list:

(a) Player's name (b) Address (c) Telephone number
(d) Age (e) Date of birth (Home & business)

★ Club staff:

(a) Title/name: (b) Address (c) Telephone number
(Home & business)

Every staff member, from the chairman to the groundsman, should be included.

★ Other information:

The name/address/tel. no. of:
(a) The local League Secretary;
(b) The local hospital (for any other than minor injuries) plus: details of lighting-up times so that the coach who is planning the part-time programme of training can utilise fully the hours of daylight; a club league and cup match fixture list to plan ahead; any other useful and relevant information.

The team manager and coach can design a personal file on each member of the squad; this will help them to monitor how the player is progressing, and generally enable them to be more accurate and objective when arriving at conclusions concerning each player. The file can contain the following details:

Medical:
A record of past injuries, number of matches missed through injury during present season, fitness tests results, weight and height measurements, general health.
Performance:
The number of first-team appearances over the season, number of goals scored or goalkeepers' 'clean-sheets' over the season, etc.
Disciplinary:
The number of cautions, sendings-off or disciplinary points amassed over the season.
Psychological:
Details of attitude to the training programme, matches, players and staff. It is imperative that the personal file is kept strictly confidential, especially if it contains information of a personal nature.

Summary:
The team manager needs to ensure by his organisation and administration that the staff have every available aid and that they are fully effective. The staff, with the team manager, must work out general codes of practice and procedures which prevent unnecessary time and effort being spent on trivial problems and leave them more time and energy for the things that really matter. The organisation should ensure that the staff work closely together and utilise fully their talents and the available resources.

2

TEAM MANAGEMENT

Taking over a new team

When taking over a new team, the team manager must not be too hasty to carry out changes. A period of adjustment is necessary so that manager and team can get to know each other, and the past experience of the players and the club must be taken into account, whether they bode well or not. The team manager is bound to be compared with the previous one and there may be a degree of mistrust or confusion which has nothing to do with the new manager but which nevertheless has to be overcome. It is vital for the team manager to get some early success with the squad, whether training, coaching, tactically or psychologically. It is best to select areas where it is relatively easy to attain early success – this will win the players' confidence. The illustration shows an example from a newspaper of how Howard Kendall, Everton team manager, engineered this. The team manager needs to analyse his entire playing staff over a period of time before deciding on his approach to them and to the squad as a whole. For example, some players may be negative in their approach so a firm line is needed, or the team may be on a losing run and as a result be demoralised – it then requires patience to build them up to the required confidence level.

Kendall gives Goodison men a 15-minute tonic

ONE goal scored against the Chinese national side in an end-of-season tournament has convinced Eamonn O'Keefe that Everton can put their name on the honours board next season.

The Goodison forward explains, "Before the match our new manager, Howard Kendall, worked with us for just 15 minutes on corner-kicks. After being two goals down we hit an equaliser from the exact move we had been practising.

"All the lads agreed afterwards that if we could score from a set piece after just a quarter of an hour's work, think what we could do over a season.

"Okay, the goal came in a match that didn't mean much. But it could just as easily have been in the semi-final of the FA Cup. You'd be surprised at how much confidence the incident has given all of us for next season.

"It illustrates the way our new boss puts things across. Every player knew exactly where every other player was when that corner-kick was taken. And when Peter Eastoe put the ball in the net it was a triumph for Howard's organisation."

Team managers change clubs regularly and some team managers do better at one club than they do at another. When taking over a new club, the team manager must find out exactly what his duties will consist of — this should prevent misunderstanding at a later date. He must also find out as much about the club as he can — i.e. its traditions, style of play and image, as they affect players, staff, ground, etc. The team manager must beware of accepting negative information about certain players which gives him a pre-conceived idea of their character and affects his approach to them. Often, players who have been out of favour and a problem to the old team manager can hit it off with the new one and find success. Ideally, it is best to take over a new club towards the end of the season, as this allows the team manager time to assess fully the strengths and weaknesses of the players, the style of play, the facilities and existing training programme, etc. He can then start to correct faults, bring in new players and allow others to go, and gradually put his ideas into practice in preparation for the following season.

Breaking up the team

Sometimes the team manager, after assessing the squad over a period of time, feels that his players are not compatible for various reasons and decides to release many of them and break up the team. The longer the team manager has been at the club the more difficult this will be, as he will have formed friendships with players and will have to tell them that they are no longer needed. It is best to make the transition gradually by introducing new players into the squad in a sensible way. Liverpool F.C. has an excellent record for producing succcessful teams over the years, thus maintaining consistency. Some team managers have failed to see the writing on the wall and have allowed veteran and ex-star players to go on playing without making provision for their eventual decline by giving younger players the necessary match experience. Timing the introduction of new players is very important, as players who stay at a club too long can become complacent.

Changing the style of play

Fear runs through almost every level of the game — the fear of losing. Soccer has become more competitive and the need to win is therefore more pressing. All team managers love to win; however, some are more concerned about not losing and they adopt a safe and cautious defensive approach with their team. Others attempt to play artistic soccer and lose regularly. The team manager must be realistic when changing the team's style of play and consider the short-term needs of the club as well as the long-term ones. For example, the team manager may join the club towards the end of the season to try to save it from being relegated to a lower division and may decide that the team needs to alter their style of play to be more defensive/attacking; this may involve a change of players' roles. He needs to be careful about this as players usually require time to adapt and older players may find it more difficult. When deciding to change the team's style of play, the following points should be considered:

The team's present situation

The team manager must consider whether the climate is right for a change and, if so, when to implement this. For example, the team and team manager could find themselves heading for relegation or they could have hit a sudden loss of form when poised for promotion. Should the team manager wait for the return of the previously successful style, or should a change be made immediately? The players, the fans or even the team manager may be getting depressed and disillusioned with the old and need the fresh stimulus of new trends.

The general character of the team

What are the players like as individuals and how do they interact with one another? Although each player has his own characteristics, the team will have a general character of its own, shaped by the stronger personalities. Older players may be conservative in their thinking, set in their ways and resistant to change; on the other hand they could be very loyal to the team manager and give the change a chance to work.

The ability of the players

The team manager must consider the technical skill, physical fitness and tactical understanding of the individuals in the squad before changing the style of play. For example, if the team manager wishes to change the defensive style of play from a zonal-marking role to one where attackers are marked tightly man-for-man for the duration of the game, then he needs to be sure that the defenders in question are able physically to cope with the extra running load; if he wishes his defensive-based rear players to come and attack more often, he must be sure that they have the necessary technical ability and skill to do so. He must not give them tasks beyond their ability.

The team manager must emphasize three factors when implementing changes to the style of play:

THE BENEFIT TO THE PLAYERS AND TEAM

The team manager must make players see the need for changing the system and must persuade them that they will benefit personally by changing. The main difficulty in changing an individual's style of play is that over the years he will have picked up habits, both good and bad. Persuading older players that the new style will be better is often difficult and requires patience. However, one thing is clear — if he wants to change the team's style of play, the team manager must change the individuals within that team.

GRADUAL CHANGE

Any changes should be made gradually. If they are made too quickly, or if too many players are changed at once, confusion will ensue. For example, team managers have been known suddenly to change a team whose style has been organised on defence into a creative all-out attacking one, often informing the players in the dressing-room just before the match starts! Players cannot be expected to cope with this sudden change in style, which means changing time-honoured methods, in a few minutes before the heat and emotional excitement of a competitive match. Before a team changes its style of play there should be much discussion, practice, coaching, and general preparation to familiarise the players with the new style before the live match.

PLAY TO STRENGTHS

Players should never be asked to perform things they are not capable of – weaknesses must be camouflaged, not exploited, for the team's benefit. Some team managers have an irrational fondness for a particular system and will try to select players to fit that system. The team manager must be realistic when changing the style of play of the team. For example, it is unrealistic to expect a winger who is known for his creative ability to spend almost the entire game defending and tackling. Players must be used on the side of the field where they feel most comfortable and where they can utilise their strengths. It may even be necessary to stop players playing the ball to team-mates in positions where their limitations may be exposed, i.e. the goalkeeper in the team may be instructed not to throw the ball out to a particular full back on his team who has poor ball control for fear that he will lose possession to the opposition in a dangerous position near his goal. Conditioned games are good for promoting this idea. When changing the team's style the team manager must make sure the players play to their strengths as a whole.

Building the team

When a team manager joins a new club, his terms of reference and responsibilities must be made clear by the Board or Committee who have appointed him. Problems between the team manager and the Board, over such things as team selections, cash and expenditure and general procedure, often emerge later in the season. It is essential to establish clearly at the start the responsibilities of the team manager, especially over building the team. It is necessary to find out how far the Board are prepared to go to gain success and what they expect. For example, they may want a stable but happy, though relatively unambitious, club where the 'family atmosphere' is all-important, rather than one which is highly ambitious and competitive. Whichever it is, the team manager should know what is required, as it may mean the difference between deciding to tear the team apart and allowing several players to leave the club, or keeping the existing players and building the team from that base. Once he knows the objectives of the Board, he can decide whether or not the job is for him. The following factors are relevant to building the team:

Recruitment

In the world of professional soccer the problems of player recruitment have become a nightmare for many team managers because of the ever-increasing transfer fee demands. The freedom to buy is conditioned by the amount of cash available and the pressure on the team manager at this stage is immense, as he has to decide whether or not the player is worth the asking price. At whatever level of the game he is involved, whether he decides that the team needs the addition of just one or two players or that it requires major surgery and the departure of several players, then the team manager has begun to rebuild the team. He will have his own ideas about the type of player he favours and the tactics he wishes to employ, but he should first take stock of the entire situation.

Gradual change

The team manager who comes to a club and immediately sets about transforming it provokes hostility from the players. He should study the players and the team, assess what needs to be done, and resolve to do it gradually. Patience is needed to tolerate those players who may not form part of his long-term plans. He may find that players who have not performed near their maximum for some time only needed the stimulus of a change of team manager to bring out their full potential. Sometimes a suggestion from the team manager that the player should change position helps him to become more successful and thus an asset to the team. The team manager may introduce new tactics, new training routines or new approaches in general, all of which have the effect of improving performance. The close season is the ideal time to make new signings and introduce them to the other players, the training routine and the style of team play. However, from time to time situations may arise in which the team manager has to make quick and possibly harsh decisions which need to take immediate effect – for example, when players have been at the club for a long time and formed themselves into cliques, which have worked to manipulate or influence other players in a negative way. If the coach can identify these players and make it clear that he is not going to tolerate a 'fifth column' within his club, then he may gain respect and make a good impact on the remaining players. In turn, they may settle down and show their playing ability to advantage.

Persuasion

Once a team manager decides that new players are necessary, his next problem is to locate the right ones and persuade them to join his club. It is not easy to do this at any level of the game, but it is certainly much more difficult at professional level where large sums of money are involved. There are various ways of finding new players; for example, individuals can act as scouts and attend matches in an organised sequence so that most players and teams in the league can be observed;

trial matches can be arranged to spot promising young players; advertisements can be placed in the local newspapers. It is vital to know which players are available and how they play. A team manager will know the type of player he is looking for, in terms of technique, skill, and physical and tactical abilities, but he will also want to know something of his character and personality. When considering a new player for his club, a team manager must ensure that he will fit in and not cause trouble by his personality or behaviour. Some form of investigation needs to be made, especially if the team manager has not seen the player in action very often. He can ask his ex-coach or team manager for an opinion, or ask players from his own team, who may have played with or against the player, or even consult a member of the press, who may have followed the player's career to date. One English League Club has been known to employ a private investigator to search out information about a player! This may be going too far, but it is important to make thorough enquiries about a new club member. Most professional clubs give any potential recruit a thorough medical test to assess his physical fitness. Therefore, if a team manager does his homework properly he will know where likely problems with any new player might lie.

Settling in

Team managers must realise that it is often difficult for a newcomer to settle in to his new club. He needs time to get used to his new team-mates, tactics, team manager, coach, training and coaching routines as well as a new environment. Patience is needed, especially if the player is recruited in mid-season or if the team is going through a bad time. Often the player is thrown in at the deep end and expected to perform miracles, when he should be allowed to settle in gradually. He will often be assessed rather critically by the team manager, coach, supporters, Board and his fellow players as soon as he is signed and therefore has to earn their respect very quickly. There are several ways in which a team manager can help the newcomer to cope with this immediate pressure. He could take the new player with him to watch the team, so that he can see how they play and how his own style will fit. Tactical sessions could be set up so that the new player can familiarise himself with the pattern of play and his role in the team. The supporters could be asked through the local newspaper to give a welcome and encouragement to the newcomer. Much will depend on the experience of the new signing; he may want to play immediately.

Team selection

The job of selecting the strongest possible team is the *major factor* in the team's ultimate success or failure, and although most people feel they can pick a winning team for any match, in reality it is not quite so easy! To do this you need experience, clear thinking, judgement, and often moral courage. The team manager must make a detailed and realistic assessment of his players and how he can mix and blend them effectively for the forthcoming match.

The team manager should consult with his assistant coaches as they

Jock Stein, the Scotland Team Manager, successfully built up the first British Club side to win the European Cup when Celtic won the trophy in 1967. The team was a mixture of youth and experience. By recruiting the correct players he achieved the overall blend that transformed the team from a good one into a great one.

will have been watching the players in practice sessions during the week and will be able to inform him about their mood, fitness, form, and any other information that the team manager requires. The team manager and his assistants should form the tactical approach for the forthcoming match, although the responsibility for the team selection must be the team manager's. There must be no confusion about this – if the coach does not agree with the team manager's choice of a player he should explain his reasons privately, but then abide by the team manager's final decision. The team manager will be under pressure from supporters, Directors, Press, to select a certain player or team, but he must try to banish all this from his mind and not let emotion interfere in any way – he must keep cool and pick the team which he feels is most likely to do well in that particular match.

The individual player performance analysis

The diagram is an attempt to analyse objectively the individual player's total performance in order to help the team manager select the team.

It will help the team manager to select his players if he breaks down their individual performances into these four parts:

The Individual Player Performance Analysis

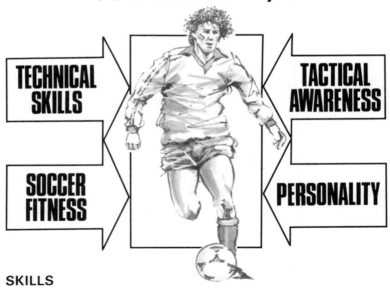

TECHNICAL SKILLS

TACTICAL AWARENESS

SOCCER FITNESS

PERSONALITY

SKILLS

The player's techniques and skills and how reliable they are in a competitive match (many players possess good technical ability but cannot produce it in the heat of the game). A player may have such a strong skill that the team manager decides to use the player to exploit an opponent's weakness, even though he is lacking in other areas. For example, he may bring back a player who has been out of favour for some time and who has good dribbling ability, to attack a full back who is known to be a poor defensive player. The strengths and limitations of each player's technical skill must be taken into account by the team manager.

FITNESS

Different positions and roles make different demands on fitness and the team manager must be sure that the player can cope with the match requirements. For example, factors such as muddy or large pitches, hot weather, age of player, fitness of opponents, role in team, will all tax the individual's level of fitness, and the team manager, when giving a player a certain role, must be sure that he has the endurance to cover the ground needed, the strength and power to give and withstand the physical contact, and the necessary speed and agility to get away from or catch opponents. The player's physique is important in some cases; if the opposing team has a tall player who is dangerous with high crosses, then it may be necessary to select a tall player who is dominant in the air to challenge him. Team managers take calculated gambles when fielding players who are not one hundred per cent fit for a one-off important match. It depends on the seriousness of the injury and whether there will be any long-term effects – if there is a danger of this, the player should not play. It should be left to the doctor and player to discuss and decide. A rigid fitness test set by the club trainer will help in making a decision.

PERSONALITY

Often team managers do not take enough account of the personality of players when selecting the team. Selecting different personality types in a team causes different reactions – get the mixture right and you will have a positive team, since certain types of player can help each other's performance. For instance, a 'cocky', confident player can encourage a quieter player to become more assured by his positive, if sometimes 'risky', play; or the team manager can select a certain type of player for a particular match where the aggression of an opponent needs to be matched or where a known nervous opponent who tends to go to pieces when beaten is there to be exploited. Players affect and influence players around them either positively or negatively. Often players will tolerate a player who has technical, fitness or tactical shortcomings if he can show by his personality and game that he can increase the team's morale and confidence. Players who are good competitors and thrive on physical, mental and social pressures can usually help other players to cope with physical challenge, and sometimes intimidation, and do well no matter what the stress. This leads on to one of the most important aspects of personality: the value of experience. There is no substitute for an experienced and 'battle-hardened' player who has been through it all before. Young players often find it difficult to adapt to the unfamiliar, whether it be an over-aggressive match, a hostile crowd, a large ground, or the opposition employing a new style of play or tactics. As a result, they tend either to drop their heads and are shut out of the game or become over-excited and lose control, penalising their team by giving away free-kicks. An experienced player will keep cool, help younger players around him and generally have a calming and inspiring influence.

TACTICS

The player's ability to 'read the game' and be in the right place at the right time, whether in attack or defence, is most valuable for the team. Players who have the soccer intelligence and game understanding to solve problems set by their opponents during the match can increase the tactical options open to the team and therefore restrict the opponents. Although the modern game increasingly requires players to be all-rounders, equally at home in defence or attack, there are always chances to use players in specialist roles, as, for example, asking a player to 'man-mark' a specific opponent throughout the game or an attacker to forsake his usual 'free-role' to become a target-man who receives direct passes from the rest of the team in advanced, but limited, positions. Some players are aware of what is happening around them and have the self-discipline to react accordingly while others, although excellent technically, do not possess the tactical know-how to use their skills effectively.

Obviously, with each of these four factors there is a degree of subjective opinion about the position on the scale of each player.

The selection of players will also decide the tactical approach to the game. For example, the slow reaction of a fullback can stifle the back four from 'pushing-out' to catch players offside and this play cannot be tried.

Guide-lines for the team manager

The team manager should consider the following when selecting the team for the competitive match:

The tactical approach

The opposition's style of play, the venue, whether home or away, the type of match, a league match or a Cup 'knock-out', or a home-and-away two-legged affair all affect the team manager's thinking. Some team managers do not believe in assessing the opposition and tell their players to 'let them worry about us', in the belief that any analysis will tend to build up fears in the players' minds about the strength of the opposition. I believe that even with the most experienced team some analysis of the opposition is important, so that steps can be taken to counter their strengths.

Play to your team's strengths

Sometimes team managers suddenly try to change their general style or system of play because of injuries or loss of form affecting key players or the team as a whole. This is fraught with danger; the team's best chance of a result is to play to their strengths and allow them to do what they are best at, whether it is to defend and counter-attack or just to attack when or where they can. The system or pattern of play which suits the talents of the *available* players must be decided on, not the other way around. For example, it is no use the team manager trying to get his team to play a 4-4-2 system heavily based on defence if the team is largely made up of attacking players. The worst the team manager can do is to ask his players to do something which they are not capable of; for instance, asking a creative player to do an out-and-out marking job on a dangerous opponent when he has neither the endurance nor self-discipline to do so, or putting a player in an unfamiliar position, say a right-sided player in the left-back role where he has to control, kick and tackle, all on his weaker foot.

The fewer positional changes that are made the better, as the more groups of players play together the more familiar they will be with their roles and each other, and the more effective the team-work will be. Gordon Jago, ex-Q.P.R. F.C. Team Manager, joined the Club at a difficult time in mid-season when his team was near the bottom of Division 2 and relegation was looming, and he immediately noticed that morale and confidence were low and the players were under severe pressure to avoid losing matches. He felt that the team's best chance was to attack, and to accept that in order to score goals they would have to give some away. As a result, the players' confidence grew and after escaping relegation they went from strength to strength.

Competition for team places

To perform to their maximum potential, players must be placed under a certain degree of pressure. Creating competition for places prevents complacency. When players sense that they will be in the team no matter how they perform, they become lazy. Leaving a player out of the team for a few matches can jolt him into starting work again and make him realise that he can be replaced if he does not play to his full potential. The size of the squad is important in providing competition for team places; it should not be so small that there is not adequate cover for the team in the event of loss of form, injuries or departures from the club, or so big that players cannot receive individual attention. The squad will usually consist of regulars, reserve players and a few promising youngsters, and if possible there should be enough players to provide competition for *all* positions.

Short and long-term selection

Some team managers select what they feel is the strongest team for each match and each player is expected to perform up to standard from the start. The team is constantly changing and the players get the message: 'Deliver the goods or you're out!'. This is not the way to manage; nearly all players, especially younger ones, require a settling-in period during which they will make mistakes as they adapt to the game at that level, and the team manager must show patience and tolerance with a player new to the team. Players do not develop at the same rate –

some can adjust quickly, some burst on the scene and fade away, while others adapt and improve gradually after a number of competitive matches. Team managers must seek consistency from their players, but must also accept that they will not always get it, especially with young players who are still developing.

Some players show great potential but will only fulfil this potential with match experience, physical and emotional maturity and careful handling – a lot depends on how the team is doing at the time. If the team is heading for promotion or relegation, the team manager will usually play safe by playing his regular, experienced players. However, if the team is in a position where there is not much at stake, he can experiment for the future by 'blooding' newcomers to the team or switching others around to play in a new role.

Timing for selection

The best time to select the team is at least two days before the match but after the final serious training/coaching session, thus ensuring that the training effort is kept to a maximum for as long as possible but that players do not lose valuable nervous energy wondering whether or not they will be playing. For maximum effect the team manager should pick the best psychological moment to inform the squad of his selection. For example, before the England v West Germany World Cup Final in England in 1966, when there was much speculation in the media about who would play in the Final – newcomer Geoff Hurst of West Ham, or Jimmy Greaves the experienced Tottenham Hotspur striker – the then England Team Manager Alf Ramsey secretly informed Hurst that he had been selected, thus alleviating his anxiety. Players should be first to know the team selection and should certainly know before the Press.

The team manager should be aware of the following negative factors which could affect the success of his team selection:

Frequent team changes

Team managers often chop and change the team when they fail to achieve success, but it is often the teams with the fewest changes who succeed, because by constantly playing together they develop better team-work. It is the old 'chicken-and-egg' question – do the defeats cause the changes or vice-versa? Sometimes the team are doing well but luck goes against them at a few critical stages in the game; then it is only a matter of time before results start to come. The players and team have learnt a lot from the opening matches, and to change things at this stage may put the team back to square one. They have overcome their teething troubles and are likely to start improving their performance. The team manager can inject energy into the team by introducing a new player; however, wholesale changes may be unwise as no pattern can form and players will feel that they are not being given a fair chance. The team manager must convince a player that he can play the new position and coach him for it.

The team manager's attitude

When selecting the team the team manager must not be influenced by the pressures being brought to bear by Directors, Press and supporters. He must base his judgement solely on the facts. It takes a strong man to do this effectively as the team manager himself can have prejudices against certain personalities, training methods, styles of play and the general way of doing things, and can let them interfere with an objective choice of player. He may have fixed ideas on how the game should be played and how players should perform and generally conduct themselves, and if they do not conform to this he is unwilling to select them, even though they are good players. For example, a player may be a quick and mobile striker, good at creating chances for others by his running, while the team manager may prefer a big, strong player in a more conservative role to act as target-man. The team manager must ignore personal likings and friendships, loyalties and sympathies for certain players when selecting the best possible team to have the best chance of winning. This will sometimes need ruthlessness since it may involve dropping a respected player, one who is a favourite with the supporters and the Press, or a player who has worked hard to get back in the team after injury. If his team is beaten, the team manager knows he will be told by many people how wrong he was!

Another problem that the team manager will have to consider is whether or not to change a winning team. Some do not believe in changing, on the grounds that it would destroy the confidence and momentum built up by winning; others believe in 'horses for courses' — taking each game as it comes and selecting certain players and teams for certain matches. Sometimes team managers do not look into the total team performance objectively enough; they become too emotionally involved in a good result and blind themselves to the fact that the actual performance was moderate.

Ian Greaves, the Wolverhampton Wanderers F.C. Team Manager, said about this problem: 'A win can hide a multitude of sins' and 'One defeat can cause panic'.

Above all, the team manager must remember that no two games are the same; the art lies in selecting the best possible team for a particular match.

The team captain

A good relationship between the team manager and the team captain and between the players and the team captain is very important to success.

Captains vary in their personalities and approach to the job, but, whatever they are like, to be effective they must get the best out of the other players. Basically, the team manager should select someone who has similar ideas to himself, and try to see that his plans are carried out by players during the game. The team manager must identify a potential captain as soon as possible and give him some responsibility with other groups of players to see how he reacts to the different players and what the players' reaction is to him. Players must be groomed for captaincy by the team manager over a fairly long period, so that when the time comes for them to take over the team they will be well prepared for the job. Many great teams had team managers and captains who worked closely together to achieve success. Some who come to mind are Sir Alf Ramsey and Bobby Moore (England), Helmut Schon and Franz Beckenbauer (West Germany), Carlos Menotti and Daniel Passarella (Argentina).

The coach must make the captain's responsibilities clear at the outset to prevent any misunderstandings. For example, if the captain changes a player from one position to another during the game and the coach does not approve, conflict may arise. After the coach and captain have agreed on the limits of his responsibility, the coach must support any decisions made by the captain.

The choice of team captain must fall on a man who is liked and respected by the majority of the team. Some captains can motivate their teams by verbal exhortation and drive while others work by quiet example. The team manager must make time to train and prepare the aspiring 'skipper' for the job, for a lot of potential troubles can be spotted before they occur by having experience of similar situations. The team manager can train the team captain by discussion and by giving him experience in handling players.

Two great Team Captains, who led their teams with confidence and by personal example, were Bobby Moore and Franz Beckenbauer seen here exchanging pennants before an England versus West Germany International match.

Just like the team manager, the team captain needs personal qualities to succeed. The following are some vital ingredients:

Leadership ability

The team captain must want to take responsibility and want to lead others by his example. He must be a determined man and have a strong motivation to win which he can transmit to the other players.

Mature attitude

The team captain must gain the other players' respect by his personality. To do this, he must be consistent in temperament and assess each situation coolly, and he must have the necessary concentration and power of command to guide the players. He must be able to keep himself in check emotionally and must control the team by knowing all his players and how they are likely to react under pressure. The captain need not be the best performer in the team, but he should be consistent because he will find it hard to lead and persuade others to play well if he is not doing so himself. Communication between the team captain and the players must be excellent.

Inspirational qualities

The team captain, by his approach and example, must be able to inspire his players often – during practice sessions as well as in matches. He must be able to inspire the nervous player and subdue the over-confident player. What is the ideal position for the team captain?

Players like the team captain to be *near* them on the field of play if possible, to give them support. Some positions are too far from the centre of activity to be effective (e.g. flanks, goalkeeper). Midfield is often considered a good position, but the average player will not have the time to see what is happening and to help others. Central defenders are usually in a good position physically to see the entire field of play and still be in relatively close contact with other positions. They will also have more time to assess play and be able to pass on information.

The substitute

Soccer, unlike some other sports, notably basketball, has not really come to terms with the use of the substitute. Players feel they are failures when substituted during a competitive match, and there have been several unpleasant incidents involving players who were substituted. These incidents detract from the image of all concerned. The team manager needs to convince his fans, his staff, and in particular all the players in his care, that the substitute can be a tactical advantage to the team and is an integral part of the game. He must make sure that all players realise the importance of the substitute. Here are some guidelines for the team manager to consider when using the substitute:

Educate the team over the use of the substitute

Before the season begins, the team manager should talk to the players about the use and need for the introduction of a substitute during matches. This talk can be communicated to the fans via newspapers, radio or television, and an explanation given of why substitutions are made – to support players. This idea must be repeated over and over again so that players gradually accept the need to use the substitute sensibly for the team's benefit.

Procedure for using the substitute

The team manager should work out a set procedure for substitutions which is sensitive and effective and saves the player's face wherever possible. The player should be pre-warned during a lull in play a few minutes before he is due to come off in order to prepare him for his withdrawal. The idea of holding up a number to indicate which player is to come off is a good one, but it should be done quickly and without fuss. It helps if the trainer meets the player as he comes off the field and into the dressing-room for treatment for injuries. If the player is not injured, the trainer should make sure the player puts on his tracksuit so that he is warm and comfortable and joins him in the trainer's box.

Integrating the substitute with the team

The substitute must feel he is a part of the team. This can be done by making sure he involves himself in the full warm-up with the other players and that he understands his likely role in the game. He must be warm and ready for action and the club should provide him with a snug tracksuit in cold weather.

The substitute as a team motivator

The substitute can be used to stimulate the team by getting him to warm-up vigorously on the side-line so that the players feel their position is threatened and consequently put in increased effort. In my opinion, this tactic has only limited use and may make the substitute feel that he is being used. Players can be substituted for a variety of reasons, for example, an injury that has slowed a player down, a loss of form and confidence, a tactical switch to cover a weakness or to exploit a situation. The team manager must also think about what type of player he selects as substitute for any one game. Sometimes he might 'blood' a promising youngster in the last twenty minutes of a home match, or he might substitute a good defensive player to defend a slender lead away from home or an attacking player in extra-time at home to try and win the game. The team manager must decide if and when to use the substitute, since if he is put on fairly early in the game and an injury occurs, the team has only ten fit men. He must also decide if a change of personnel will upset the team system and rhythm or be a boost to a flagging team.

Dropping a player

The team manager often has to make unpopular and unpleasant decisions which result in players being dropped from the team to make way for others. The way this is done is very important, as the manager can end up either with a partially placated player who accepts that his form has not been good or with an angry player who feels that he is being made the scapegoat for the team's lack of success. The team manager may drop a player for a variety of reasons, such as loss of form, tactical reasons, injury or lack of match experience. He will need courage and tact to do this, as the player in question may be the type who always gives one hundred per cent effort. The following guide-lines will help:

When and how to drop a player

A major problem for the team manager is deciding *when* to drop a player. To drop a player after one bad game is to admit bad judgement in selecting him in the first place. Does one poor performance mean the chop or should the player be given more chances to show what he can do? The team manager must be objective and pin-point exactly why the player produced a poor performance. It could be for a variety of reasons, such as his team mates performing poorly and thus affecting his own play; an early mistake which destroyed his confidence; illness or a slight injury. Players are more likely to be resentful and angry if they are dropped without warning or if they feel the decision to be unfair in some way. In general, players are not dropped because of one poor game; usually they are going through a period of indifferent form. The team manager must then tell the player that his form is inadequate and that he must show improvement in certain areas of his game, so that when he is dropped he has at least had some indication of why. Whenever possible, the team manager should let the player know *before* anyone else that he has been dropped, since to hear the news from a team mate, a newspaper, or another source can only be bad for his confidence. By informing the player discreetly that he is being left out for the forthcoming match, the team manager allows the player himself to tell his team mates or others; this is better for his self-respect.

When is the best time to inform players? This will depend on a number of factors, such as the need to select the team in order to commence coaching for a forthcoming match, or whether the team manager has his full complement of players or is waiting for fitness reports on others later in the week.

Motivating players to get back in the team

Players will differ in their reactions to being dropped — some will get angry, some depressed and some will accept the situation and fight hard to get back in the team. The team manager must treat each individual accordingly and must support them to some extent without allowing self-pity or unrealistic excuses. Ideally, the player should feel concern for the team. Reports on his second team matches will be studied closely by the first team coach, and his attitude to training should also be assessed at this time. The team manager should inform the player that if he does his job on the pitch, he cannot be kept out of the team — it is up to the player to rebuild his confidence and game. Sometimes a team manager will drop a player who has become complacent and feels that his position is assured no matter what happens — the sudden jolt of being dropped from the team, especially if the team does well without him, may push him to better performances. This should not be done often, and careful thought must be given to the likely consequences.

Summary:
The team manager needs to be able to make clear-cut and correct decisions on all the team problems that might confront him.

3

THE PARTNERSHIP OF COACH AND TEAM MANAGER

The roles of the coach/team manager are many and varied depending on the club and available resources and staff. At some clubs he will take no part in some roles, but in others he will either take direct responsibility or delegate the job to another member of staff.

It is widely accepted today that one man cannot deal adequately with all the duties required in the running of a soccer club. Many successful clubs have partnerships where the coach and team manager work together in their own particular, but inter-related, areas to get the job done. The two partners must work in harmony and must co-operate to show a positive 'face' to the team. The team manager must work out areas of responsibility for the coach and delegate accordingly, remembering that he can do this only if he trusts and believes in his coach. Often the team manager has known the coach for a long time; problems can arise when a coach is unknown to the team manager. A good relationship is vital to the team's success. The team manager must get as much information as he can about the coach before deciding whether or not he is the man for the club. It is a good idea to arrange one or two meetings to establish his philosophy and ideas on tactics and approach to the game, attitude to players and to sportsmanship. Eventually, a general picture will emerge. There are often disagreements and differences of opinion between the team manager and coach; this is natural between people who are highly motivated and work closely together in what is often a stressful situation. They may differ over the tactical approach to adopt, team selection, disciplinary methods and training programme. Much confusion can be avoided by forming simple 'working rules' and sticking to them. It is vital that there is an honest, hard-working and co-operative partnership between the two men, for success on the field can be achieved only by successful preparation off the field. Many successful partnerships have been a combination of different, but complementary, personalities. The team manager should not always go for a coach who is similar to himself. A contrast can often be more effective when dealing with the players, for often one man can get through to some players better than the other, and vice versa. Often one can balance the other's extremes of personality. For example, a team manager who is volatile, tends to be too emotional at times and chastises players after a match can often provoke a negative, angry reaction from them. A coach with a quieter personality can have a calming effect on the players and the situation can be restored to normal. When selecting the coach this aspect must be considered.

Although their personalities and approach to the job can differ, their basic ideas must be the same otherwise frictions are bound to occur and cracks will eventually appear in their relationship. For instance, if the team manager condones foul play by turning a blind eye to it and the coach believes in winning by sticking to the rules, they have a serious problem in their different approaches to the game. If they both agree that one of their players should be punished for consistent foul play, they may approach it in different ways (e.g. the team manager may give the player a mild ticking off and fine him a smallish sum of money, but if it were left to the coach, he would let the player know in no uncertain terms what he thought of his conduct and suspend him from training and the next match). The approach is different, but the basic philosophy is the same. This particularly applies to coaching and whether or not the team manager is a coach. I have seen team managers hire a coach even though they do not really believe in coaching! It is unrealistic for a coach to work all week preparing a team to play in a certain way for a forthcoming match, and then for the team manager, who has not been with the players, to select a team and ask them to play in a completely different way from that which the coach has been encouraging. This is obviously unsatisfactory, but it has been known to happen. Ideally, the team manager should have coaching experience and do some coaching work with the players so he understands the problems and principles

Dave Sexton, the Coventry and England U21 Team Manager, is seen here observing a match. He is an accomplished coach who spends much time on the training area with his players so that he does not become isolated from them but rather is in a better position to make managerial decisions such as team selections. As a result he is always familiar with the team's form and playing pattern.

involved in developing players and teams. The team manager and the coach should be working with each other rather than against, especially with regard to team selection.

Guide-lines

Share responsibility

The team manager should encourage the coach to give his opinions on things. Some team managers feel that if the coach does this he is directly criticising him. If he does not give the coach the opportunity to air his views, the latter may resent the fact that his contribution to the club is being limited. If the coach feels strongly about something he should be able, without recrimination, to disagree with the team manager's opinion and to state why. The team manager must make the coach feel that he has an important part to play and that he is using all his ability to the full. The coach must be given the authority to do the job and the team manager must support him without looking over his shoulder every five minutes. The amount of responsibility given will obviously depend on the experience and ability of the coach and the degree of trust the team manager and coach have built up during their time together.

Work to strengths

Both the team manager and the coach should work to their strengths for maximum effect when delegating responsibilities. If the team manager is also a good coach he may involve himself in a greater proportion of coaching work so that the team have the benefit of two coaches during their training programme. If the coach is a good communicator he could handle the Press, and be responsible for some public relations work.

Solidarity

As has been mentioned, the team manager should encourage free exchange of opinion with the coach but with one proviso – differences of opinion are *never* aired in public or in front of the players. The coach may disagree violently with one of the team manager's decisions; however, provided he has the opportunity to explain his objections to the team manager, it is his duty to carry out the team manager's orders whatever he thinks or feels. To let the players sense otherwise lets the team manager and their relationship down. The team manager must have the final responsibility for all decisions as he is the one who 'carries the can' when things go wrong. A united front must always be presented to the players, otherwise they will start to lose confidence in the staff.

Coach and team manager types

To be effective with players, the team manager and the coach must each understand their own personality – its strengths and weaknesses

44

and how it is likely to affect the majority of players. This can be very difficult as everyone has an inbuilt defence mechanism which goes into action when criticism is implied. As a result, people tend to overlook their own shortcomings, or else they justify their behaviour by blaming something or someone else. If experienced and responsible people find it difficult to come to terms with their own failings it will help coaches to understand how much more difficult it is for younger players to admit weaknesses which they have ignored for years! Coaches' and team managers' personalities, just like their players', differ a great deal; it follows that their particular styles and methods will also differ. Some are flamboyant and brash, others are quiet and studious, some are talkative and direct, and so on.

Model of Coach/Team Manager

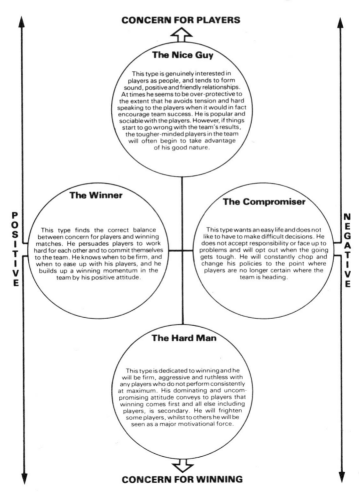

CONCERN FOR PLAYERS

The Nice Guy

This type is genuinely interested in players as people, and tends to form sound, positive and friendly relationships. At times he seems to be over-protective to the extent that he avoids tension and hard speaking to the players when it would in fact encourage team success. He is popular and sociable with the players. However, if things start to go wrong with the team's results, the tougher-minded players in the team will often begin to take advantage of his good nature.

The Winner

This type finds the correct balance between concern for players and winning matches. He persuades players to work hard for each other and to commit themselves to the team. He knows when to be firm, and when to ease up with his players, and he builds up a winning momentum in the team by his positive attitude.

The Compromiser

This type wants an easy life and does not like to have to make difficult decisions. He does not accept responsibility or face up to problems and will opt out when the going gets tough. He will constantly chop and change his policies to the point where players are no longer certain where the team is heading.

The Hard Man

This type is dedicated to winning and he will be firm, aggressive and ruthless with any players who do not perform consistently at maximum. His dominating and uncompromising attitude conveys to players that winning comes first and all else including players, is secondary. He will frighten some players, whilst to others he will be seen as a major motivational force.

POSITIVE

NEGATIVE

CONCERN FOR WINNING

Success and survival, in many cases, demand that the team manager and the coach produce a squad which wins more matches than anyone else. It is a fact in soccer (particularly higher in the League) that if you do not produce consistently good results, you do not survive!

The previous model shows four of the major team management or coaching types and their characteristics. This provides a guide-line for the team manager or coach to assess and study his own style.

Basic attitude to winning and losing

The team manager and the coach are assessed mainly by whether their team wins or loses matches, regardless of how the result is achieved. This puts a lot of psychological pressure on them to cut corners and to win by whatever means they can, justifying themselves by blaming the referee or the other team for starting the trouble, etc. The coach/team manager must be completely honest with himself and assess his feelings about winning and how to approach losing. Often, winning is the only thing that matters and a team manager/coach is obsessed by this to the exclusion of everything else, including the team's performance. He should question his motives, and ask himself, 'How far am I prepared to go to win? Am I prepared to ask my players to cheat and bend the rules?' Team managers/coaches often talk about the need for a code of sporting practice between each other and the players, but, like the players, they find justifications during the heat of the game to forget the code. The reasons for this are understandable. The team manager or coach closely identifies his team's success or failure with his own personal success or failure; therefore, if the team loses, the coach automatically becomes a failure. The coach/team manager must take some share of blame for a defeat just as he takes a share of credit for a victory. In defeat he must think clearly about what went wrong and how it can be corrected for the next match. For example, it may have been the team selection, tactics, or team performance on the day. This does not mean that the team manager/coach should take defeat lightly! The team manager/coach who does not feel disappointment at losing lacks commitment and eventually the players will sense this. Generally, the coach/team manager's conscience will tell him whether or not he is breaking the sportsmanship code – although it will be particularly difficult to be sporting when he and the team are under the constant pressure of being on a losing streak!

The role of the coach

The main objective of the coach is to produce the most successful team performance in the shortest possible time, and then maintain this over the season. The coach can have a powerful influence on the team, and the interaction between him and the players is important to the team's success. Usually the coach is closest to the players and with them most often, and the interaction depends on how the players respond to his personality and methods of working. The coach must not be a blackboard theorist – he must be a practical man who constantly sets up realistic and stimulating practices which encourage players to learn new skills and tactics and keep the established ones in trim. The coach is the 'data bank' who stores knowledge and experience which can be utilised instantly for the players'/team's benefit. The expertise and skills that a master soccer coach requires are considerable and include:

Analytical ability

The coach must be able instantly to isolate and analyse the key factors in technical skill or tactical play.

Demonstrational ability

He must be able to give clear and realistic demonstrations which show the players the problems in question and ways of overcoming them.

Practice

He then needs to be able to set up effective practice situations so that the players can carry out many successful repetitions of the skill or tactic in question until it is integrated into their game.

For example, the coach must find out why a player who normally dominates opponents with strong but fair tackles suddenly starts to mis-time them, or why passes which are delicately flighted are intercepted, or why the goalkeeper allows shots which he would usually stop with ease to beat him, or why a team seems unable to keep possession of the ball.

Players need help in these situations and that's where the coach comes into his own. To do all this the coach needs to have knowledge and practical understanding of the following areas of coaching:

★How the brain transmits messages to the muscles of the body, and how the body reacts physically to perform the skill.
★ The key factors in technical skill and tactical development.
★ The laws of the game.
★ Principles of soccer skill learning and coaching.
★ Human behaviour, group dynamics and psychological principles of playing the game of soccer in competitive circumstances.

He needs also to have the administrative and organisational ability to use his knowledge effectively.

The role of the team manager

The aim of the team manager is to motivate and guide all the relevant staff, players and resources to maximum effect. The higher you go, the more problems you encounter and the more competitive it becomes; therefore the more pressure there is on the team manager to produce results. Directors, staff, supporters, players, Press, can all be directly or indirectly on the team manager's back when the going gets rough. The team manager has to see a wider picture than the coach and make sure that all the key factors are working harmoniously to gain success. He will be on trial by public and players alike, and will be judged on how he confronts situations and what decisions he makes.

To be successful, the team manager will require the following personal qualities.

Moral courage

The team manager will need this in abundance as the pressure on him to succeed will be considerable, whether it is to change his style of play, team selections, or training programme. Ron Greenwood, the England International team manager, showed moral courage of the highest kind for years when in charge of West Ham between 1960 and 1970. He withstood constant pressure from all quarters to change his team's approach from an artistic and skilful one to a more rigid and aggressive one in order to win more matches. He refused to do this and continued to promote 'classical' soccer, whatever the outcome. The team manager should try to keep things in perspective — he must be a realist and remember that he is only as good as the players he has. Success is relative: a coach who can keep his team in mid-table when they looked doomed to relegation may be doing a better job with his players and resources than a coach who wins a league championship with a group of highly talented players. Often the team manager will have to make harsh decisions, but if he feels they are right he must make them and be prepared to face the consequences.

Consistency

Soccer players, like anyone else, feel most comfortable with situations and procedures that they are familiar with. The team manager must try to show consistency in his dealings with players, general policy and planning, as to constantly change things will only cause confusion.

Dependability

The team manager will find that making difficult decisions, such as 'dropping' players, will be easier if the players trust him. Trust has to be earned over a long period — it certainly will not happen overnight. The team manager will be assessed by the players in a number of ways, some quite subtle. For example, he may be asked for something to be allowed, and it may seem to be of a trivial nature, but he will be assessed on what he decides. The team manager could be asked if he can remember to fetch something for a player on a match day — he may be tested on his reliability and trust. A golden rule is never to make a promise that you cannot keep, no matter how small. Some team managers promise things and then forget them or find out that they cannot fulfil the promise. If in doubt, it is best to say you cannot do it in the first place. The team manager must be dependable at all times.

The team manager's experience and expertise in the following areas are important to the team's development.

★ Attention to detail.
He must be able to establish the best way of operating and be one step ahead of the others in his quest for success.
★ Ability to communicate.
The team manager must be a good communicator and be able to talk effectively to his staff and players.
★ Organisational ability.

He needs to be a good organiser and ensure that all the club's resources are used to maximum effect through minimum effort.

The team manager needs to know what are the key factors in all aspects of team management and work and plan to ensure that he makes correct decisions, as far as possible, on the problems which will confront him. He will need knowledge and experience of the following aspects of team management.

★ How to talk to and counsel players, both in one-to-one and group situations; to overcome grievances; and to pass on ideas and information.
★ Up-to-date information on the current advances in tactical play and the form, strengths and weaknesses of the opposing team and players in his team's particular league as well as the opposing teams in cup matches.
★ Administrative expertise; to cut down the time-consuming chores of the job and to keep his involvement in meetings, letter-writing, telephoning, organising travel to and from matches, and money-raising schemes to a minimum.
★ The modern team manager has to be aware of how public relations can affect his job and club. He needs to show tact in what he says and how he says it, in order to build up good relationships with supporters, sponsors, the local press and other media.

The player/coach or team manager

Some people are hired to do two jobs: be a player and a coach or team manager at the same time. Some players have been successful in this dual role, others have not. Some can inspire when on the field of play and can affect other players quite significantly by their presence; others, usually ageing players struggling with their own performance, have neither the playing ability nor the personality to inspire their players. Some are good on the field of play but lack the general managerial/ coaching know-how to do the job off the field. Ideally, of course, they can do both jobs well.

The player/coach/team manager, when playing, must see that he does not try to do too much and take responsibility for everything and everybody. The team manager in charge of a player/coach must treat him like a player when talking to him before and during the match, at the half-time interval, and at the post-match inquest. The player/coach must accept this and not become involved in disagreements with the team manager. A player/team manager must give full responsibility to his coach to make the decision to substitute him or any other player and must leave him in charge. If the player/coach/team manager is still a good performer and can inspire others, and if he has a sound working relationship with his coach/team manager, the combination of roles can work well.

Physical and mental fitness

The team manager and coach must see that they maintain their health and fitness, as the job requires much energy. They also need to be mentally fit, for they will be emotionally involved with the team. Since they do not have the same opportunities as the players to get rid of their tensions, they are apt to suffer more mental stress. Things can get on top of them temporarily, e.g. domestic problems, illnesses, disharmony and worries with players — these all build up tension. However difficult it might be, they must not let their problems get through to their players. Generally, soccer coaches seem to be able to 'switch off' and forget their problems and concentrate on the job in hand. Sometimes a coach may lose his temper with a player without a good reason. If a team manager/coach does erupt due to his own personal problems he should apologise to the player when he has cooled down or as soon as possible after the incident. Usually players will understand that tension can build up in coaches and that they are not infallible. The apology will often gain the coach respect and not be seen as a weakness. This factor is important because he will often be assessed by players on his personal fitness and his capacity to deal decisively with stressful situations. If the team manager/coach is overweight and unfit, he should take steps to correct this situation — even to designing a short but gradual diet and schedule to lose weight and build up his general fitness. He does not need to be as fit as his players, of course, but he will win their regard if he can show them that he can involve himself in the coaching and training programme. It must be remembered that coach/team managers spend long hours outside in the cold and wet weather and take a lot of criticism which could affect them emotionally. They will be able to deal with these problems more easily if they are in good health. Don Howe, the Arsenal F.C. and England coach, has a daily personal fitness programme which he adheres to fairly rigidly.

Summary:
The main aim of the coach is to provide the correct learning atmosphere for success, as without this he and the team will struggle. He needs a positive personality, a good knowledge of the game and how to set up realistic work that will directly affect his players. The team manager must prove himself in the competitive world of soccer by the difficult and different decisions he has to make with the staff and the team. Their success depends on how well they co-operate to achieve these various aims.

4
COACHING

To win League Championships, and to be consistently successful over a period of time, a coach must prepare his team thoroughly by hours, months and years of high-quality, intensive practice. It is easy to identify the worried coaches who dart about just before the match giving the players last-minute instructions which they cannot possibly assimilate at that time. Such coaches merely transmit their anxieties to the already nervous players. Good coaches do all their work during the week to prepare their players for the stress to come in the actual game.

Coaching session model

The coach must develop his coaching expertise, and design and conduct his coaching sessions on sound psychological principles, taking into consideration the following factors.

Coaching Session Model

PLANNING

OBSERVATION ← **ORGANISATION** → **COMMUNICATION**

MOTIVATION

(Learning)

Planning

The coach must plan the session carefully to achieve maximum effect on his players and team. All too often coaches go out to the session with nothing specifically planned and go through the motions believing that the players will improve anyway. Nothing could be further from the truth! Possibly in no other area do coaches break so many rules of training than in planning their coaching session. Often the practices which the coach has set up for his players have little relevance to their needs as a team or as individuals, and only serve to disappoint them when they are in the competitive match. The coach should design a Coaching Session Plan Sheet and have it duplicated for use at each session, with the following details included – objective, number of balls, posts, etc. Writing details on paper helps the coach to memorise the essential material that he wishes to convey to his players. If he wishes, he could have his written plan on a small card which he could carry in his pocket. As long as the coach does not refer continually to his card, he will not lose the respect of his players.

Session No: _____ **Coaching Session Card** **Date** _____
ORGANISATION CHECKLIST

Players			Equipment
1	9	a	
2	10	b	
3	11	c	
4	12	d	
5	13	e	
6	14	f	
7	15	g	
8	16		

Session Objectives:

1. _____   2. _____

2. _____

3. _____

Warm-up

4. _____   3. _____

Comments: _____

If the coach charts and records all sessions, he can assess and analyse what went well and what did not. The plan should not involve the coach in much administrative work; it should be simple and to the point.

Organisation

Ideally, the coach should have a few minutes to himself before the session in order to gather his thoughts, prepare himself mentally and set out the practice area required. The players will appreciate this and it will allow the coach to start productive work immediately. The group must be organised and controlled quickly so that they can listen to instructions and see any demonstrations given by the coach. This is difficult if the players are scattered over a wide area or if there are distractions and they cannot see or hear properly. The coach should make sure that all his players are close together (preferably sitting or kneeling), that they are not playing around with footballs, and also that the sun is not shining directly into their eyes. He should ensure that if there is a brisk wind he speaks with his back to it so that his voice carries to the players. The coach must be able to set up a demonstration using himself or a group of players to show what is wanted. Once the players fully understand the lesson in the demonstration, a good coach allows them to play and practice what has been shown. The next stage in the coaching programme is observation.

The author gets his players' full attention before starting the coaching work.

Observation

Once he has organised the practice to his satisfaction and the players are working effectively, the coach must observe carefully to see what more he can do to improve individual players and the team as a whole. If the result is not what he intended to demonstrate, it could be that he has not organised and designed the practice correctly and he might need to modify his practice layout. The coach's position at practice is important. Sometimes he will need to be in a wide position from which he can see a large number of players over a large area – for example, where the subject is 'team tactical play'. At other times he will need to be close to an individual or a small group of players to see exactly what is going wrong and how he can help. The coach should not be involved too closely or for too long in a practice; he will lose effect this way. It is better for him to stand back to see what needs to be done, before going in to make his point quickly and clearly and then moving out again to a wider position. What the coach observes will depend a great deal on his experience and knowledge of the game. He can see best what is going wrong by looking from different angles.

Communication

The coach communicates ideas to players through their eyes and ears. It is important that he should not talk too long or too quickly as players will lose interest. Generally, players learn more from seeing than hearing. They do not like to listen too long to detailed explanations of why they did not perform correctly, they prefer to be *shown*. The coach must demonstrate (on the field of play where possible) rather than talk about the problem. Time must not be spent talking about things which occur in the game, but which do not have much relevance to the topic in the practice session. Instead, he should emphasise the key factors concerned. The coach's speech and how he uses his voice are important in getting his ideas across to players, and also to their acceptance of them. The voice can be used effectively in a variety of ways to convey different things to a player. For example, sharp and loud to give direct orders; quickly and enthusiastically to motivate players; in a calm, slow fashion to quieten excitable players.

Motivation

This factor is in operation throughout the three previous stages and it is imperative that the coach realises that no matter how good he is in the other three areas, if he cannot motivate himself and his players to practise to improve their performance, the outlook for him and his team must be bleak. The coach's presence is very important to the degree of effort and concentration that the players show in the practices. The coach should move around from unit to unit, motivating players by spending some time with each one whenever possible to help overcome any faults. If players feel that the coach is always with them at each practice session, they are more likely to work to the maximum.

Supervision of players

Often the coach has to leave a group of players by themselves while he works on another group or on an individual player. This is where problems can start, as only the most conscientious players will attempt to practise properly. Others will work half-heartedly or even fool around and as a consequence develop bad habits which will undermine the work being done by the coach. What can the coach do about this? He should, whenever possible, leave an assistant coach, the team captain or a senior player whom the players respect, in charge of the group. He must try to motivate the players to work on some aspect of play or even to play at match speed by involving them in some sort of competition with incentives for the winning team. The coach must make it clear to the players that he will find out the result when he returns and he must use his ingenuity to ensure that the practice is as successful as possible.

Model of System of Work

Stage 1:	DEMONSTRATION	Example
	The idea from game situation or from the best match played.	The coach decides that the team requires concentrated work on basic defensive play. He sets up a match or phase of play to show players what needs to be done and where they are going wrong.
Stage 2:	COACHING	
	Set up realistic practice groups whether individual, group or team to coach technical skill or tactics	Players are broken into 2 v 1, 2 v 2 groups etc. Situations in the grids so that they can experience early success and concentrated repetitions of a simple nature. For example - learning how to stop attackers from turning, etc.
Stage 3:	PROGRESS	
	increase the complexity of the work by increasing the Number of players and speed of practice, gradually bringing it nearer to the full competitive match.	The practice can be moved from the grids to the area on the field where the action takes place. Players are grouped in 3 v 3, up to 6 v 6.
Stage 4:	GAME	
	Depending on the main objective the game can be 6 v 6, 8 v 9 or 11 v 11.	When the players can cope the coach must work on 11 v 11 using various methods to teach players to understand basic defensive play in the game.

It is not necessary or practical to work from stage 1 to stage 4 in one or two sessions — the coach must decide when and how to progress, as going too quickly can be as bad as going too slowly. A lot depends on the topic, how the players are coping, and what they are ready for next. Some of the stages in the diagram can be omitted and the players can go straight to the full 11 v 11 game situation, as some of them feel that practices and drills involving small groups are not really related to the game. The coach must diagnose what is going wrong with the team or players and set up the appropriate practice programme to improve them in the most efficient way and in the shortest time.

The effect of fatigue

Nearly all fitness work of a heavy nature should follow, not precede, the skills and tactical coaching work. Fatigue affects the players' muscular and mental co-ordination and their capacity to think clearly and make correct decisions. This in turn makes it very difficult for the players to perform their skills (particularly the light touch ones like ball control) and the reading of the game. The players must be relatively fresh in mind and body so that they can receive, absorb and memorise the information given by the coach. Occasionally, perhaps once a week, the coach can organise a session where the players are given the fitness session first and then go straight into the skills or tactical work in order to train them to maintain their skills and tactical performance, even when heavily fatigued, just as they have to do in the competitive game. However, he should only do this with players who have well-established skills.

Controlling the practice session

The coach can start and finish the practice himself; however, sometimes this can make it difficult to observe well. If a player is used, he should be able to perform the desired skills (e.g. crossing the ball) and he should be directed by the coach to where he wants the ball served. Beware of the practice becoming a pressure practice by restarting the service before the players are prepared; it is best if the players can walk back to their respective positions before the next service starts. The other players must know if the server can join in the practice after serving or if he has to remain where he is. It is a good idea to serve the ball in a variety of ways and from several positions by having a few servers positioned at different places. For example, the servers can be positioned centrally or on the flanks in different thirds of the field – all this adds to the realism of the practice. It is also necessary to maintain control and continuity of practice by having ball retrievers where possible (esp. shooting practices) to avoid delays.

Coaching methods

To obtain the maximum benefit from a practice session the coach must have the skill and perception to use whatever coaching method is most effective and productive for the squad in each particular coaching situation. He must also have the experience and flexibility to be able to change the method according to the circumstances. For example, on a cold, wet day it would not be desirable to use a method which necessitates having to stop play frequently and where players have to stand and listen to instructions while feeling cold and damp. Similarly, it is unsatisfactory to work on individual techniques with a large group of players when there are only one or two footballs available. The coach must think about the method(s) he will use when planning the session and the probable effect it will have on the team's play. Remember that although many coaches appear to have a 'favourite' method, no one method is best. Much depends on the expertise of the coach. He must consider the following four areas before deciding on the method(s) to use during his coaching session:

The Objective
What is his intention? To improve skills, physical fitness or team-work? Is it for individuals, a group, or the whole team?

The Players' Attitude
What is the team's general attitude to coaching? Are they energetic and keen or dull and apathetic? Are they on a winning or losing run of matches? All this will affect their attitude.

The Weather
Is it a cold, wet, humid or hot day? What is the state of the training surface?

The Facilities
What are the total facilities available? What pitches and practice-areas does the team have? Are they working indoors or outdoors? How many players are there, and how many footballs, coaching bibs, poles and additional aids are available?

The coach can be further guided by the following analysis of the major coaching methods in use today:

Method 1: Freeze-Play

This method is one where the coach instructs the group of players to freeze physically as they are moving and playing, by verbal command or by the use of a whistle, to focus their attention on a particular aspect of play.

Analysis:
The 'action-replay' idea of stopping play and re-creating the situation clearly shows even the slowest-thinking player what is happening and so works at all players' speed of learning. The clever coach can get his players involved more fully in the learning process by asking questions

Freeze-Play

The Coach has 'frozen' play. He may now encourage B to come inside with the ball while A overlaps him on the flank.

which force them to think and come up with the answers to the problems, thus reinforcing their reading of the game. On the negative side, if play is stopped too often it can irritate players and kill motivation, especially if long discussion between coach and player ensue. The coach must also be very perceptive and experienced at freezing play at the right moment and re-creating the situation as it actually happened, otherwise disagreements can occur; the coach will lose credibility in the players' eyes if he does not get the facts right.

Summary:
This method can be a very effective one if used properly, i.e. when introducing a new tactic where play needs to be stopped fairly frequently in the early stages until the players have incorporated the new tactic. Gradually, play needs to be stopped less and less. The coach should be as brief as possible when freezing play and should not talk too much or re-create an incorrect situation (especially on a cold or wet day).

Method 2: Condition-Play

This is where the coach stresses a particular aspect of play to the group by constant repetition. He narrows down the players' choices all through the practice so that eventually they can perform only that particular apsect of play. The conditions can be imposed by changing the rules of play (e.g. by altering the dimensions of the pitch so that it is narrower or wider, or by allowing each player two touches before he passes the ball). Players can be further conditioned by the use of incentives in the way of praise or points for performing the aspect of play correctly or by deterrents such as free-kicks or points deducted for failing to incorporate the features concerned into their play.

Condition – Play

The teams are playing 6 v 6 soccer on a reduced pitch with the condition that the attacking players must all be in one half of the field for the goal to count. This develops compact team play.

Analysis:
It gives players the opportunity for repetitive and realistic practice of major aspects of play and helps to develop team-work. The coach can leave the practice session unsupervised to some extent in the knowledge that the conditioned game will ensure some learning is taking place. From the negative point of view, too much condition-play can restrict players' thinking and form bad habits by unrealistic play. Furthermore, it can deter players from learning new aspects of play by putting too much emphasis on one particular part of their game.

Summary:
This method can be very effective for emphasising key factors of play to the team. Condition-play should not be used for too long and the 'conditions' should be changed according to the team's needs. Finally, the coach must make sure that the conditions are as realistic as possible, and that the rules are simple.

Method 3: Drill-Work

This method involves small groups of players practising techniques and skills, with or without opposition, by constant repetition and movement. The coach must think carefully about the number of players he puts in each group, because if too many are used, there will be a lot of inactivity.

Analysis:
This is a good warm-up method where players get many repetitions of the skill or technique in order to develop or maintain it. The coach can also put more emphasis on fitness if he so desires by increasing the speed and distances that the players have to cover. Finally, it can help to reinforce key match situations for players. On the negative side, drills employed by coaches often bear little relationship to the actual game or else they are done at too slow a pace to improve the players. Some drills are confusing to players and they can narrow their thinking if done too often or for too long.

Drillwork

The players are practising a basic wall-pass drill which ends with a shot at goal.

Summary:
Drills are good for warm-ups while still maintaining the players' skills or techniques and also for 'lighter breaks' in between the hard spells of physical work, and they help to break up the monotony. To be effective, drill-work must be done almost at match speed and as near the realistic game situation as possible. The coach must avoid complicated and entertaining 'circus-acts' which look good and which players may quite enjoy, but which will teach them nothing about the authentic game.

Method 4: Directing Play

This method involves the coach in giving verbal instructions and advice to the players during play to help them identify the correct actions in given situations and to get them out of bad playing habits.

Analysis:
Can help players to improve their vision and game understanding to some extent and also eradicate bad habits. But one coach's voice constantly talking to the player can irritate him and make him become robot-like in his play. It is very difficult for the coach to time his calls correctly so that they coincide with the players' actions and decisions. The opposition knows what to expect and the method may also give the players too much to think about.

Directing Play

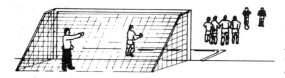

The coach directs the goalkeeper to set up his defensive organisation against a free-kick.

Summary:
This method is limited; however, it can be useful in reinforcing ideas and eradicating features of poor play.

Method 5: Repetitive Pressure Play

Generally, for coaching purposes, repetitive pressure play is designed to improve techniques and skills by working very fast, so that players react quickly as they would in a match, and react with accuracy when their limbs are heavy and their powers of judgement are beginning to fail. By designing the practice so that players have to run often and at speed without adequate recovery intervals, the coach can work on fitness. Usually the practice is arranged so that the players receive a continuous supply of services and barely have time to play the ball before the next one is served to them. The work-period should be timed so that players do not work flat out for longer than 35–40 seconds – the skill factor will usually suffer if it carries on for longer than this.

Experience indicates that players do not usually work flat out in these practices and work-periods of one minute can be given so long as the service, work and rest periods are well controlled.

Analysis:
This method can help players to control their nervous state when involved in reaction-type skills, (e.g. shooting or quick passing, etc.). The player can learn to keep his techniques and skills going much better when fatigued. Finally, it is easy to organise in groups and the players can be motivated by comparing results. They also tend to enjoy this type of work.

Repetitive Pressure Play

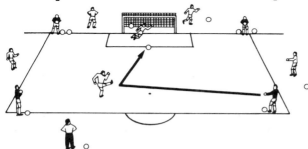

One player's shooting techniques are put under pressure by four feeders who give him continuous service in rotation.

Summary:
A good method for keeping players on their toes, but used wrongly it can break down a player's skill as continual playing for any length of time will eventually result in fatigue and loss of accuracy.

Method 6: Shadow-Play

This method is one in which a group of players or team play against an imaginary opposition or a few opponents where they are heavily outnumbered. Some coaches use conditioned-play like two-touch to try and bring it nearer match speed. Claims are made by some coaches that it is very helpful in developing tactical play and systems of play for the team without the pressure of opponents.

Analysis:
It can be useful as a 'refresher' occasionally from heavy work, as a warm-up, or to practise restarts when only a small number of players are available. From the negative point of view, there may be little transfer from training to competitive match level unless the coach believes that skills and tactical understanding can be developed without the use of opposition. It requires a lot of motivation from the coach and it can also create bad habits because it does not oblige the players to make the necessary decisions that playing against opponents requires.

Shadow Play

White players rehearse free-kick options in shadow form. Flagposts represent the defensive 'wall'.

Summary:
Coaches who use this method regularly during the week with their players are likely to be disappointed with the team performance on Saturday afternoon, as indeed are the players. It does not present the situations that players encounter during the 'live' match, and for this reason it has a very limited role, although, in my opinion, it is good for the initial stages of tactical practice.

Method 7: Functional Practice

This method involves marking out a realistic area on the playing field and using a small group of players with the objective of increasing one or more attackers' or defenders' understanding of their positions and tactical duties in the team and their relationship with others around them.

Analysis:
This method creates rapport between players and coach as they feel they are getting individual attention from him. It also helps players to understand their tactical function in the team. From the negative point of view, it depends on the motivation and co-operation of all players, which sometimes can be difficult. It also needs a lot of attention from the coach which can be very time-consuming.

Functional Play

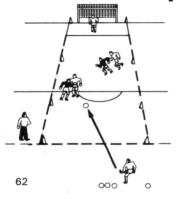

Play is 2 v 2 down a narrow central channel. The coach can work on the strikers' or centre backs' functions.

Summary:
This can be good for helping to develop confidence in players by working on major weaknesses which may be hindering them. As soon as improvement is shown by a player or small group of players, it should be incorporated into a more advanced stage which involves more players and is nearer the match situations.

Method 8: Phase Play

This method is the natural progression from functional practice, where the emphasis is on much larger groups in an area at least half the size of the pitch, working on an attacking or defensive phase of play.

Analysis:
It can be effective in developing team-work in difficult team units and understanding of roles amongst groups of players. The practice is neatly spread between realism, repetition and match play to make it quite exciting for players. It is then easier for the coach to focus on either the attack or the defence rather than having to give his attention to both where he might not involve them so fully. One disadvantage is that the defensive players not directly involved in the coaching work can become bored by having to repel attacks with no end in sight, or the attackers not directly involved can become demotivated by stoppages which prevent their making progress. The nature of the practice can make players adopt unrealistic positions when the practice starts from the servers.

Phase Play

The prior functional practice has been enlarged to one third of the field where defence plays attack. The service starts with one of the central players receiving the ball.

Summary:
This method is good for squad-work when there are 14—16 players and the coach can involve them in fairly realistic play which is motivational and can help team-work.

Method 9: Coaching Grids

These are a series of squares or rectangles marked on a pitch or on a piece of ground, where convenient, usually measuring 10 × 10 m square. The coach can use them in a very flexible fashion to work on different aspects of play by joining them up to make various combinations of areas to accommodate groups of players.

Analysis:
This method is good for helping the coach's organisation and for accommodating large numbers of players meaningfully. It is also good for working in detail with individuals or with small groups. On the other hand, players often find difficulty visually, in relating the grid-area to the actual field of play, so they feel it is artificial. Over-used, it can make players play their game 'too short' unless longer play is encouraged.

Gridwork

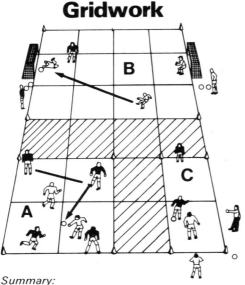

Grids are used to give meaningful practice to the squad, e.g. 4 v 2 possession play; shooting and goalkeeping drills; 1 v 1 dribbling practice.

Summary:
Provided players are educated to the need for grids, they can be effective in developing techniques, skills and basic tactical play by graded practice. They are also flexible, and the coach can organise small games, skill tests, fitness work, etc., as well as the more conventional work; however, as soon as progress is seen on the grids, the players should be put on the normal field of play area as soon as possible.

Method 10: Coaching in the Game

This method is where the coach employs one or a combination of the other coaching methods mentioned to coach one or both teams in the full 11 v 11 game situation.

Analysis:
Probably the most effective transfer of training situations, provided players are at the required level and the coach is adept and experienced enough. Good for facilitating team-work and tactical understanding and also for preparing players for the full competitive match. Negatively, if the match becomes too competitive it can spoil the coaching theme, so the teams learn nothing.

Coaching in the game

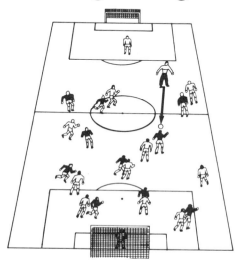

In an 11 v 11 game the Coach sets up an attacking situation from the defensive third of the field.

Summary:
This method can be too complex for players who require 'graded' help to overcome their particular weaknesses and who may require other practice situations. The coach must be experienced and, for this method, he must be able to work well and motivate the players; however, it is generally the most effective method when used by a good coach.

Obviously there will be some overlapping of the use of the ten major coaching methods, but generally these guide-lines will help the coach to pitch his practice sessions at the correct level and give his players maximum benefit from his expertise. The coach needs to plan a coherent and effective programme which brings each player and the team to their maximum potential.

SOCCER SKILL LEARNING

To be effective the coach must know and understand the processes by which players learn to play soccer, as by knowing what is happening in the player's mental and physical make-up, he can accelerate the learning process. If the coach does not know what should happen psychologically, he will have to rely on trial and error methods which is not very satisfactory.

Principles of skill learning

Motivation

The player must want to learn before he can improve as a player. Some players have a driving desire to learn while others are not so keen and need stimulating and pushing to reach their maximum potential. The coach must design his practice sessions so that players are interested in what they are doing and experience success during the practice. These sessions should be varied as there is nothing more boring than doing the same thing day after day. Sometimes players (particularly young ones) play the fool because of lack of variety and challenge in the practice sessions.

Transfer of training to the competitive game

To have maximum impact, the practice which the coach sets up must be as near the competitive game as possible. This means close observation by the coach of the tactical situations, skills, techniques, physical movements, workload and mental stresses of the game. Players must practice in the conditions which they will encounter in a match; for example, on varied pitches that might be hard, muddy, icy, of irregular surface and small in size. Players must experience playing the game and maintaining their concentration when cold, fatigued, in rain and snow, or playing under floodlights. The coach must ensure that players play in the correct footwear and with the correct size and weight of football wherever possible, to ensure transfer of training. Many coaches, concerned about the possibility of their players being injured in practice, often prohibit normal tackling or slow down the speed of the practice in order to reduce risk of injury. By doing this he prevents his team from practising realistically for what will confront them in a competitive match. After they have learned basic skills and tactics of the game, increased pressure should be put on them gradually until they can produce these skills at match speed. At practice, the coach must always encourage players to play at full match speed and also to challenge for the ball as they would in the actual game.

The coach must always have transfer of training in mind when preparing a coaching session and include each week an 11 v 11 practice match in order to gain maximum transfer of training.

Players' participation

The coach will increase the players' understanding of the game if he involves them personally in what he is attempting to do. Players will be motivated if they are involved and told what and why they are practising and what the coach is trying to achieve. In this way, the coach will make the player see the relationship between the practice situation and what happens during the competitive game, thus aiding the transfer of training. The coach must always encourage his players to question and discuss things with him and, equally, he must listen to what the player has to say. Often players have positive suggestions to make which will benefit the player and team. The more that players participate in the practice sessions, the more likely they are to retain these ideas in their minds.

Practice

Football techniques, skills and tactics are best learned and developed by repeated practice. The length of a practice session will depend on the interest or mood of the players, the weather, the time of day, the degree of fatique. All these factors can influence the effectiveness of practice. Often coaches pack too much into a session and end up confusing players who cannot take in all the information and therefore lose interest. A good maxim for the coach is 'quality of practice is more important than quantity'. It is better to do a little well, than a lot badly.

The best response from players is obtained by shorter periods of intensive work involving maximum mental concentration and 'game-like' physical effort, followed by short recovery intervals with a change to lighter and more entertaining activities with the ball. For example, a practice session spent mainly on improving the system of play affords little time to improve individual techniques and skills, whereas a session spent on basic skills with individuals will do nothing to help group or team understanding. Coaches often cannot agree on whether it is best to work from the 'whole-part-whole' or from the 'part' to the 'whole', the whole being the game, and the part being a smaller part of the game. It depends on the coach, the players he has at his disposal and the practice environment, as sometimes players cannot see the relationship between the part situation or the game situation and thus the practice is not effective. Often, from the players' point of view, it is better to start from the beginning, i.e. with a full game (this could be the last match that the team has played), and the skills or tactical theme that the coach wants to practice with the players can be taken out of the game so that the players can all see clearly what and why they are practising.

Reinforcing ideas

Often coaches make the mistake of thinking that because some aspect of play performed in practice or in a match was successful, this will always be the case. This simply is not true, because individual and team performances will fluctuate, and players tend to forget things that brought them success earlier unless they are constantly reminded of them. Coaches must remember that players are individuals; some have better memories than others and can retain information easily, whereas some will need more revision of lessons learned. By continually going over important aspects of play, players will understand and memorise situations from the practice session and try to apply them in the competitive match. The coach can aid players' understanding and ability by constantly reminding them to ignore irrelevant details which will do nothing to improve their play. He should focus their attention on the things that really matter and emphasise them by repeated discussion and demonstration.

Players need constant repetition before aspects of play are learned and integrated into their playing system. But although repetition is important in coaching, it can restrict players' thinking and performance if practised on too narrow a theme, for example, in playing 'phase-play' where the back four unit of the team are constantly 'conditioned' to deliver long passes up to two central strikers without much variation.

Treat players as individuals

The coach is making a serious mistake if he treats all his players in the same fashion, as they have different temperaments, habits and needs, and must be treated on that basis. Some will grasp ideas more quickly than others. Some methods and approaches will work better with one player than with another. The interaction between the coach and the player is very important. The state of mind of player and team will ebb and flow depending on the circumstances at the time. Players will react better when they are winning. This is the time when the coach can safely give the players more work, as players will be in the right frame of mind to practise and work harder. Players who are part of a team which is on a losing run must be treated more delicately, as they will be much more difficult to motivate because of loss of confidence, depression, staleness and, perhaps, frustration and anger. The following guide-lines will help the coach put these principles into practice.

Guide-lines for the coach

Desire to learn

The coach must convince the player and team that he needs to improve some aspect of play and also persuade them to accept his methods of achieving this. The coach must use his personality to sell the idea to his players so that they can see that they will benefit from the new skill or tactic. For example, if a player is a good attacker but neglects his defensive roles, the coach must convince him that both he and the team will benefit from a change of role. To do this, the coach must make the player see what it will do for him – perhaps in gaining him more esteem from his team-mates, or gaining praise and support from the coach, or having the ball to do more of the things he most likes doing, such as attacking.

Practice at match speed

As practice progresses and the players' and team's abilities and understanding improve, the coach must gradually introduce methods which duplicate competitive match situations. Early practices should be relatively free of pressure, either by the coach's interference or by the difficulty of the task. The coach should increase the intensity and speed of the practice, depending on the rate of progress of the players, and he can do this by having the players involved in competition against themselves or other team-mates, or by being given 'targets'.

Assessing progress

The coach must be able to measure the improvement or decline of individual and team performance over a period of time, so that he can assess the impact of his work. The coach can assess his team in a variety of ways – match analysis, evidence of goals for and against, etc. However, the ultimate test for the coaching and training programme must always be the competitive match, whether assessing individuals or the team. If what the coach has worked on with a player or with the team during the weeks of practice turns out to be right on match day, the practice has been a success and the player or team had gained maximum transfer and fully understood the work introduced by the coach.

The need for patience

Both coach and players will need to show patience when learning a new aspect of play. The coach must make players understand that there may be quick success when learning a new skill which will be followed by a period when, no matter what the player does, nothing seems to improve. Some coaches often panic and change their methods of approach too soon during this period; instead, a coach must have the courage and patience to give his players and the new aspect of play the necessary time to improve, for if the idea is sound and the coaching method is correct, it is just a matter of time before the player improves. Sometimes the coach must be prepared to see the performance of a player or even the team suffer in the short term in the confidence that they will improve in the long term. Individuals vary in the rate of learning – some forget things more quickly than others, some lack determination and lose heart easily, and some are prepared to work for a long time in the belief that they will improve. In such circumstances, players must be assured by the coach that provided they are patient and keep trying, success will definitely follow.

Distractions to learning

To be effective, the coach must be aware of, and try to get rid of, as many distractions as he can for himself and the players in order to get something of value from the practice sessions. The following factors will all affect practice sessions from time to time.

Fatigue

This affects the capacity of the players to make the necessary movements, to perform the technical skills, and their ability to concentrate and make the correct decisions. This is particularly important when introducing new skills or tactics.

Noise

Noise will interfere because the coach will not be able to communicate correctly if he cannot be heard. On the other hand, the coach can shout too much, as can other players involved in the practice. Players who are learning new skills or tactics, particularly younger ones, are often intimidated and confused by too much noise and consequently their performance suffers.

Over-coaching

In the early stages of learning, it is usually necessary for the coach to be heavily involved with the players, giving a lot of verbal and visual guidance. However, as soon as the players show signs of understanding and progress, the coach's involvement can be reduced gradually. A coach can make too many decisions for players so that they become too dependent on him. Players must not be so rigidly controlled that they cannot think for themselves, because during a competitive match they cannot rely on the coach.

Atmosphere

The weather, whether wet or dry, windy or humid, will affect the mood of players. The time of day, the training pitch or surrounding area, and the general mood of the team will affect the training atmosphere. Often coaches try to battle through a theme when it is apparent that the players are not receptive. It may be that the coach has not created the correct atmosphere by his manner and methods, or it may be that the players are in a particular mood and he has failed to see that the theme needs changing.

Lack of motivation

The players must want to succeed and learn before they start to improve. If the players come to the session apathetic, the coach must find ways to arouse and motivate them so that they wish to get involved in the practice session. The coach can use whatever methods he thinks best; however, the use of suitable incentives and rewards, competition and attractive practice work – say, with the ball – are usually effective to this end.

Inhibitions

It has been mentioned earlier how the coach can inhibit players, particularly younger ones. The same applies to older, more experienced, ones who stifle the education of younger players by intimidating them to the point where they are afraid of trying new things. The older players often exploit the youngsters for their own benefit when they should be encouraging them to be creative and opening up the options for them. Working groups comprising the right blend of older and younger players can eliminate such difficulties.

Technique and skill

The difference between skill and technique, and how they are developed, has caused some confusion amongst soccer coaches over the years. Let us first try to define what they are and how they differ.

Technique:
This is the ability to execute a solitary action in isolation from the game – for example, a type of pass, shot, a side-step or dummy or a catch. The player can develop his individual techniques by practising against a rebound surface on his own. The mental decisions involved are minimal and are concerned only with *how* to perform the action of heading or passing without the distractions of other players.

Skill:
This is the ability to be in the correct place at the correct time and to be able to select and use the correct technique on demand. Unlike techniques, skill involves the player in making decisions relating to opponents and team-mates during the game, so the environment is more unpredictable.

Some players have a wider range of techniques and can make the ball 'talk', displaying excellent control and touch; despite this, however, they cannot utilise these techniques in the 'moving' game and therefore cannot be deemed to be skilful soccer players. Technique, therefore, is only a part of skill. The player has to be able to apply technique and skill in the heat of a competitive match where physical challenges from opponents afford little space or time for decisions and where the situation is constantly changing.

What does this knowledge mean for the coach?

★ When diagnosing a player's performance, it should be established whether faults are of a technical or skilful nature and appropriate action and practice should be set up.
★ Players must be coaxed and encouraged to display a wide range of techniques by good demonstrations.
★ In my opinion, players at all levels of the game should be given the opportunity to practice techniques individually when the practice session begins, without the hindrance of opposition. Youngsters particularly, or even older players who are practising a new skill or technique, should do this without distraction to gain early success and confidence.
★ As soon as improvement is shown in the player's performance, increased stress must be put on execution of techniques. This can be applied in a variety of ways, i.e. quickening them up, increasing the number of repetitions, more accuracy by giving less space, or by technical competitions.
★ The amount of time and the level the coach works at will depend on two main factors:
(a) whether he is working with an unsophisticated learner to develop the new technique, or
(b) whether he is working with good technical players and the objective is to maintain and rehearse existing techniques.
★ When the players are technically competent they must be put in a situation involving co-operation with team-mates against opponents, either playing away from or towards a goal.
★ The coach must set the level of practice for his player. This should not be set too low but should allow plenty of time for practice and gaining the confidence needed to reach the required standard of performance.
★ He should finish the practice session with a conditioned game to test the newly acquired techniques and skills in the smaller game and the full 11 v 11 game. Finally, it is always a good idea to end with an uncoached and unconditioned game.

Soccer skill

Soccer is a game where the players' contribution is concerned with on-the-ball and off-the-ball play, and the making of decisions in an ever-changing environment. A considerable amount of research has been done into what happens during an actual game in terms of play and the following facts have emerged:

The following diagram shows that in an imaginary 90-minute match, e.g. between Liverpool F.C. and Everton F.C., the ball will be in play only for approximately 60 minutes. The ball will be 'dead' and out of play for 30 minutes because of delays caused by restarts and stoppages in play of one kind or another. (These figures are approximate.)

In the 60 minutes of actual play in an evenly-balanced match, both teams will have possession of the ball for 30 minutes.

Each player in the team will have actual possession of the ball for a longer or shorter duration, depending on their position in the team and their involvement in the game; however, the individual, on average, will

not have the ball for longer than two minutes.

This means that the player, whether goalkeeper, rear defender, midfield player or striker, will be moving about the field for 58 minutes without the ball. Approximately half of that time will be spent defending and the other half attacking for his team. Whatever his function during that time, he will constantly be making decisions and judgements about how he can best help his team – e.g. 'how close should I get to mark this man?', 'should I cover a dangerous space or man in this situation?', 'can I draw a player out of position to allow my team-mate space?' or 'can I get away from my marker to receive the ball from a team-mate?'.

It is easier to spot and appreciate what a player does on-the-ball, but more difficult to recognise good off-the-ball play. Both are important in recognising and developing skilful soccer.

Analysing technical skill

As has been mentioned, for the larger part of the game the player does not have possession of the ball, therefore he spends his time making decisions about how best to help the attack/defence. When he has the ball he decides on what to do to attack correctly. So whether he has the ball or not, there are three stages for the coach to analyse when deciding what needs rectifying when skill breaks down.

What option to select from the alternatives available

Did the player select a reasonable option? Was a pass 'on' or should he have held on to the ball? Did he pass to the wrong player? Did he allow himself to be drawn out of position to mark an opponent, leaving a dangerous space for the opposition to exploit?

How will I do it?

When the player has decided what needs doing, he then decides how he is going to do it to achieve his first objective.

Technical execution (when)

After deciding how to do it, he needs to execute the correct technique at the correct time for the situation. Here are some examples:

ATTACK

On the ball
A winger with the ball on the flank:
(a) decides to cross the ball into the penalty box area.
(b) decides to cross the ball to the near post area.
(c) performs the technical execution needed for the cross.

Off the ball
A striker awaits a throw-in being taken by one of his team-mates:
(a) decides to decoy a certain defender away from an area of field.
(b) decides on how to do it — calling for the ball and check-out movement.
(c) executes the run and takes the defender with him.

DEFENCE

Off the ball
Full back sees play approach him:
(a) decides to cover team-mate.
(b) decides how to do it. Leaves his immediate opponent and considers his angle, distance and position.
(c) executes his action to get in the covering position.

Off the ball
Goalkeeper in goal area sees a cross coming in high from a flank:
(a) decides whether to go for ball or stay on goal line.
(b) decides to go — calls to defenders and decides whether to punch or catch.
(c) executes his action.

Skill can break down at any of the three levels and it is important that the coach realises that the player needs help in making the correct decisions, whether of a technical or a skilful nature, and this can be done only if the coach understands and identifies what is going wrong. Technique and skill are inter-dependent, to a large extent. For example, time after time a player may fail to give a 25–35 m (30–40 yd) pass to an unmarked team-mate on the other side of the field. One reason may be that the player on the ball did not have the ability to 'get his head up' and perceive the team-mate, even though he might be an excellent all-round passer. The second reason could be that the player could certainly see the unmarked team-mate, but elected not to play the pass (which could have led to a goal for his team) because he did not have the confidence to execute the necessary technique with accuracy over a distance of 35 m (40 yd) so instead he played a shorter and more negative pass. The coach can see from these examples how limitations in technique can limit players' skill.

Peter Shilton, the former Nottingham Forest and England Goalkeeper, demonstrates the need for quick and correct decisions in clearing a high cross with a one-handed punch despite the challenge of Cyrille Regis, the West Bromwich and England striker.

Experience

The player uses his past experiences to help him make decisions in a competitive game. For example, a striker is about to receive the ball with his back towards an opponent and has to make the decision quickly on whether he should pass the ball first time, hold and screen the ball, or turn with the ball. He will tend to base his decisions on how successful he has been in the past in his response to this situation – 'feedback'. He may have tried to turn with the ball a few times before and found that he did not have the necessary control, speed or timing to elude his marker – so he cuts out that option. Often younger players make more elementary mistakes because, unlike more experienced players, they do not have the amount and variation of soccer experiences to draw upon. This is where the coach is vital. He can pinpoint important ploys and actions, thereby leaving the repetitive movements to match play.

Physical and mental processes

Each time a soccer player displays his skills or responds to situations, certain physiological processes take place which the coach must understand.

The player sees a situation and decides to react. The mind sends messages to the muscles telling them they must act. The nerves are like telephone wires along which impulses pass to the various muscles of the body, and the speed at which the individual player can pass on these messages differs from player to player and largely depends on whether or not he was born with fast reflexes. When the message comes to the muscles, two things can affect reaction. Firstly, the state of preparation of the muscle (sometimes called the muscle tone) is important. It should be ready to spring into action and can be prepared by a good warm-up and the correct mental concentration. The second is for the muscle to be as well developed and powerful as possible. Some players are very strong but are slow in movement and lack power relative to their bodyweight, while others may not have a great strength but can use what they have with more speed and they are therefore more powerful.

The brain

The statement that 'soccer players have brains in their feet' may sound good, but like many cliches it does not give an accurate or realistic account of the role the brain plays in the game of soccer. For example, a striker breaks clear of the defence with the ball at his feet in a race towards goal. The sort of information coming in to the player could be: 'should I go all the way on my own or look for a team-mate approaching?', 'have I the speed and strength to beat the recovering defenders?' or 'how near are they to me?'. The player will see the goal get nearer and may see the anxiety on the goalkeeper's face for a fleeting moment, he will hear the crowd shout and will feel his nerves tighten. He may notice a muddy area on the edge of the penalty area and decide that he should take avoiding action. Through good training the striker may store some of this information in his memory-bank for future reference; this is termed 'feedback'. Other bits of information may be discarded by the brain as being irrelevant to the situation e.g. an opponent who can be seen out of the corner of the player's eye but is too far away to disturb him. He then acts quickly.

The nerves

Movement is caused by electrical impulses transmitted by the brain to the muscles via the nerves. Each message 'burns' a microscopic passage which makes it a little easier to repeat the message, movement and skill next time. Many thousands of repetitions develop a so-called 'groove' or habit – it's just as easy to develop or groove bad habits as good ones and very difficult to eradicate bad habits which have been well grooved. It is important therefore that the coach sees that players practise correctly at all times, so that eventually players can trust their brains and bodies to repeat the technical skills and responses of the game automatically and 'free' their minds to think about more immediately important factors, such as tactical reading of the game, analysing opponents, and the state of play. The less skilled players always seem to be fighting for control of the ball and have to do things in a hurry,

Skilful players, on the other hand, often have better physical 'touch' and control and greater anticipation, therefore they have more time available and greater freedom to execute their skills accurately.

Habits (Good and bad)

Many people in soccer talk about players developing 'good habits'. What do they mean by this? Many of the player's technical skills, movements and responses can be quickened and conditioned so that the player performs them almost without thinking. There are dangers in this sort of learning, however, for if a coach ingrains into a player the wrong response to a situation, it is difficult for the player to get out of the habit. For example, a player may play the shortest and easiest pass that he sees each time he has the ball, when it is obvious that more effective passes are open to him; or a full back, seeing that his winger has the ball, suddenly bursts forward on an overlap run down the flank time after time, using up precious energy and gaining no advantage for his team. Both these stereotyped responses may be the product of bad coaching. The soccer player needs to be able to make speedy decisions after examining the situation building up around him. For example, a midfield player in possession of the ball in the attacking third of the field may have to decide whether to pass, or hold the ball and wait for more support, or go it alone and try to shoot at goal. He has fractions of a second in which to make his decision, otherwise he will lose possession of the ball and the attacking opportunity will be lost to his team. A player can be trained to make speedier and more accurate decisions incisively by cutting out bad habits, for example, selfish play, giving away free kicks or penalties, bad tackling or being caught in possession. The coach must attempt to replace bad habits with good ones. All this needs his patience and sensitivity.

Performance model

The simplified model below of the physical and mental processes involved in human performance gives an idea of the functioning of the human system. The system basically works like this: the player sees a situation and information from what he sees is relayed via the sense organs to the central mechanism of the brain. Here it is sorted out and decisions are made on what needs to be done in a particular situation. Finally, the appropriate muscular response is made and the player performs the movement in order to execute the technical skill or tactical action required. Feedback can be utilised by the player immediately or can be stored in his memory for future use. The coach is very important to the player's knowledge of how he has performed, for example, in the technical execution of striking the ball or in his tactical response to a situation where he was defending with two attackers approaching him and his goal with the ball at speed. The player can make errors either by selecting the wrong information from the situation, or by interpreting the information from the sense organs incorrectly, or by timing the muscular movements incorrectly.

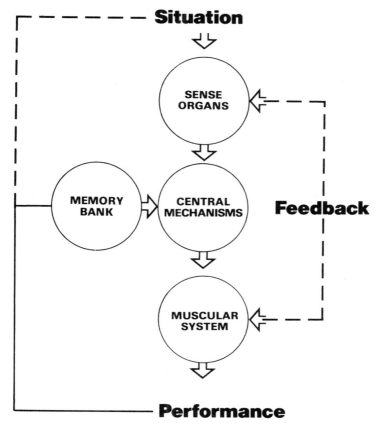

Steve Coppell, the Manchester United and England winger, and Kenny Dalglish, the Liverpool and Scotland striker, display the need for alertness, concentration and controlled aggression as they contest a ball during a British Championship match. Coaching practice must help players to develop these mental qualities as well as the physical ones.

Demonstration

Coaches need to get ideas across to players quickly. The ability of the coach to set up meaningful demonstrations is a most important part of his job and he should note the following factors:

Clear picture

The old maxim that 'one picture is worth a thousand words' is often true, and very much so in soccer coaching. The visual demonstration gives a quick and clear picture which can be repeated over and over again. The coach should go through the demonstrations at different speeds for the sake of clarity.

Motivational

If the demonstration is a good one, it will often have a motivational effect on the players who will wish to practise so that they can repeat and learn the skill for themselves. It is important therefore that the demonstrational model is a realistic and effective one and good performers should be selected for this reason.

Key factors

The players should be helped by the coach to identify the key factors in the performance of the skill by the use of verbal information given in a brief and effective way. At the first demonstration, it will be difficult to

All eyes are on England and ex-Ipswich Team Manager Bobby Robson as he demonstrates a point to his players.

focus players' attention on technical points as they will tend to look at the skill aesthetically as a whole. But gradually they will accept technical information about the skill.

Exactness

The demonstration is a model for the players or team to copy until an acceptable level of competence and performance is achieved. The coach must allow players to develop their own natural responses, comply with principles which suit their physical and mental make-up, and not merely ape the demonstration.

Proof

The coach must always be ready to prove his ideas, and demonstrations can be used effectively to show sceptical players that good coaching develops skills.

Summary:
The coach must understand the physical and psychological principles by which players learn to play soccer as errors in his handling can greatly retard the player's ultimate progress and development.

6

MOTIVATION

The coach can have a considerable motivating effect on his team, depending on his personality and his understanding of how players feel and react, and on the methods he uses. Too many coaches treat players as if their brain is separate from the rest of their body; such coaches know little about how motivation affects players. They think that certain factors will affect players in their team in the same way, which is not always the case. It is relatively easy to get players wound up for a match; it is another to motivate them to such a degree that their confidence, aggression and enthusiasm is at its maximum. A player who is physically very fit will normally have a positive attitude to training and matches. However, he may not be keyed up correctly for the match and as a result will perform badly. Almost all human beings have the potential to respond easily to crude forms of motivation, especially in situations when they are anxious about the outcome of a forthcoming event. In these cases, it is relatively easy to encourage players to become over-aggressive, angry, or downright hostile. Many clubs have suffered from the 'fix bayonets and charge' motivator, who looks upon the game as a battle with no room for ethics and where anything goes. To be effective, the coach must teach players to come to terms with their psychological weaknesses and strengths as well as their technical, tactical and physical ones in order to control them effectively. The personal motives of the coach are important in that only by understanding his own motivations can he understand what effect they will have on his players. The coach must ask himself – and answer honestly – the following questions:

★ Why am I coaching?
★ What do I want from my players and the game?
★ What are my standards of sportsmanship?
★ How important is winning and losing?
★ How do I expect the game to be played?

All motivation is personal, and many players lack consistency of performance for a variety of reasons which may include lack of confidence, over-aggressiveness, timidity, anxiety, lack of concentration, or fear. These mental blocks prevent the player from performing at his peak and to overcome them the coach must find out what causes them and seek to remove them so that the player can fulfil his potential. A soccer coach can watch a player go through the motions in a morning training session, or observe him during a club practice match and be completely unimpressed. The same evening, before a crowd and in the competitive match, he looks like a worldbeater – the first two routines had failed to motivate him but the evening match did. The almost universal belief that professional soccer players are highly motivated because of high financial rewards is not necessarily true. The basic drives towards improvement in the game were established when they were youngsters, long before the earnings incentive was apparent. All players have the capacity to improve psychologically, but, as with skills, fitness and tactics, it requires patience, sensitivity and understanding from the coach. The coach who uses his players to boost his own ego by satisfying unfulfilled ambitions, or by trying to work out his own character flaws through them, is thoroughly misguided and will surely run into trouble if he does this.

When considering motivation the coach must accept that all players are different, and although most will respond well to conventional methods of motivation, others will require a different approach.

Principles of motivation

Player involvement

The coach will get more from his players, and increase their understanding of the game and confidence, by involving them in everything he does where possible. He should explain not only *what* to do but *why* they are doing it, so that the players are involved mentally and physically in such things as team talks and asking for individual opinions of how to overcome problems.

Organised training session

Nothing demotivates players more than a session that is disorganised and lacks balance of content. The programme should be well planned and should cater for the individual group's and team's needs by giving them chances of success during the session and also ensuring that the players have sufficient variety of activities to keep them involved. Generally, players who are highly motivated and want to improve do not need as much variety as players who are not so motivated and cannot, or will not, concentrate for long periods on what the coach is doing. This type of player needs a change of activity fairly often in order to maintain his interest. The key motivator in soccer practice is the ball!

Setting objectives

The coach must, whenever possible, give his players something to aim for and motivate them to greater efforts. The coach must get to know each of his players well, for without knowing their fears, ambitions, etc., it will not be possible to set effective objectives for them. Short and long-range 'targets' should be set with suitable incentives if the targets are met. The coach must set objectives that are worth the effort for the players and which will benefit their play in some way. He should design these so that each player or the team experiences early success, but gradually the objectives should get more difficult to achieve, so that the players are continually being stretched. Objectives can be set for players to score a certain number of goals per month or season, make a certain number of first-team appearances as a 'newcomer' to the squad, or for the team to amass so many points within a certain time to get more possession of the ball in their matches. Competition against himself or against team-mates within the training programme, if used properly, can help a player to improve and reach his objectives. Incentives are most important to the players and must be used carefully by the coach. He should find out what incentives motivate which players most, e.g. pride in one's performance – doing better than others, financial or material incentives, or more esteem among team-mates for increased performance. The incentives must be commensurate with the importance of the objectives set, and should not appear trivial to the players.

Training atmosphere

Wherever possible, the coach must try to create an attractive learning and practice environment for his players. The atmosphere around the training area should be as free from noise and distractions as possible to allow players to concentrate. The area should be attractive in terms of a bright dressing-room, and flat, grassy and marked areas, as there is nothing worse for a coach and his players than a dark, cold, wet and depressing training area which will dampen everyone's spirits. All equipment should be laid out so that it has visual impact for the players. The general training atmosphere will also be affected greatly by the current individual and team form. There will be a severe loss of confidence if they are losing regularly, and this is where the coach must be at his best and work hard to persuade players to 'get their heads up'. He must show courage by identifying himself with his players, to demonstrate that he supports them and shares in their defeat with them. It is only human to dissociate yourself from a losing team, but nothing could be worse – for players and the coach. They must not blame bad luck, wallow in self-pity, or become angry or depressed; instead they all must accept responsibility, find out what is going wrong and put it right. There are not many problems for the coach when the team is winning – everyone wants to play and train. However, the coach must beware of complacency when things are going well; he must remember that things will not always be so good! The coach should look out for this with his players and himself and keep one step ahead by pushing the players and keeping the momentum going.

The coach's personality

All the above-mentioned principles of motivation are of secondary importance to the coach and how he organises things. A good coach can make a drab dressing-room come alive and can also make the training field an enjoyable place on which to practice. His manner will be his own; however, he must be positive, relaxed and firm when necessary and be able to lift his players when needed. He should set examples of appearance, conduct and punctuality to his players and will earn their respect. He should also get to know his players by talking to them where possible, at each session, if only a few words. The coach should talk about things such as family, friends, ambitions, interests, etc., as this will build up the trust and respect of his players. Nearly all players have known coaches for whom they would run through brick walls! This respect is not due to a coach because of his position – it has to be earned over a long period. The coach should be an enthusiastic and inspiring leader of men and the players will follow his example if they respect him.

Guide-lines for motivating a player

When attempting to motivate players to improve or change some aspect of their game, the coach must consider two basic approaches:

★ *Persuasion* – The coach informs players about how the change could improve them and appeals to the attraction of success.
★ *Direct approach* – The coach tells players what to do in a firm and definite manner.

There is little doubt that players need, and even like, to be 'pushed' at times, but not too often. Too much of this will lose players, especially if done in a threatening manner. Generally, players have to be convinced of an idea, rather than forced to accept it, for it to be effective. However, the coach can use both approaches, depending on his players and the situation, with effect.

To motivate a player effectively the following steps are recommended:

Emphasise his strengths

The coach should start by mentioning something that the player can do well which will make him more receptive to the information to follow. He should be sincere in his praise; he will lose credibility if he tries to tell the player he is good at something which he knows he is not.

Suggest the idea

When the coach feels the player is reasonably receptive, he should suggest the idea to him, as clearly as possible, telling him where he is going wrong and how he might be able to put it right.

Plan of attack

Get the player to focus on the problem and decide how to attack it by joint consultation. He must set objectives for the player and assure him that with effort and patience on *both* their parts he will improve. For example, the coach might use these three steps:

Argentinian Team Manager, Caesar Menotti, talks persuasively to Diego Maradona who listens attentively. Instructions should always be positive, concentrating on what the player can do, rather than what he cannot do.

Coach: 'John, your tackling and winning of the ball was great on Saturday. I think you could make it even better if you played the ball to your team-mates a bit sooner, rather than tending to slow down the game by holding on to the ball before releasing it; in this way I think you would catch defenders out more before they get back to recover. What do you think?'

John: 'I've never noticed this in my play, and I'm not too good at playing the ball quickly.'

Coach: 'I'm not asking you to play the ball early all the time, just sometimes when it's 'on' – it will improve your game. I'll plan a few weeks of practise where we will work on this aspect of you seeing the early ball when it's 'on' and playing it – let's see if you can improve this one thing, John – O.K.?'

Motivation in training

The basic problem for the coach is how to make a period of physical and mental stress an interesting and productive experience for the players. The players should come to the session with some eagerness and should not treat it as a necessary chore. The coach can assess the effect of his coaching programme by the manner in which the players continually approach the session. If they are dull and apathetic, the coach will have problems and needs to re-assess his programme. The coach's dream is for players to come to the practice session full of zest and enthusiasm to learn – this can be produced by a carefully-planned motivational programme, with the presence of the coach at each practice session.

Guide-lines

DEMONSTRATION – A good demonstration can often motivate the player or team to try to repeat what they have just seen. The demonstration can be done by the coach or another player, or by taking an example from a previous match or a television excerpt.

TRAINING TARGETS – Players like competition and also like to know how they are doing in the session. The coach can record scores and achievements on charts, record cards, etc., showing such things as times and number of runs, number of goals or points, etc., for different groups.

NOISE – The coach can use his voice to increase the volume of noise to stimulate players, or he can incite other players to shout and encourage their team-mates to increased effort.

USE OF 'SPECIALISTS' – No matter how good the coach is as a motivator, the players will become bored with the same face day after day. The coach can introduce a new face to work with the players for a spell (e.g. another coach, lecturer, club doctor, etc.). Working with an outsider can stimulate the players, especially if he is experienced in his field and has rapport with the players. Many top English League clubs have used the expertise of athletic coaches to improve player fitness and motivation. The coach must ensure, however, that the work the specialist does with the players fits in with the programme and does not conflict with his work in any way.

INCENTIVES AND DETERRENTS – The coach can use conditioning to motivate players by giving them incentives to do well and deterrents to stop bad play or lack of effort. Ian Greaves, the ex-Wolverhampton Wanderers F.C. Team Manager, devised such a system within his club and uses it, for example, to reward players who shoot on target by loud praise, while 'punishing' players by continuous shuttle runs for shooting off-target. The coach must be careful how he uses this and must never 'punish' a player who cannot perform a skill.

Sustaining motivation

The coach must provide sound leadership which transmits itself through the team captain to the squad of players, and sustain motivation over the playing season. Coaches vary in their personalities and in their style of motivating, e.g. some have a dynamic approach while others are quieter and more thoughtful. I am constantly being made aware of the different ways that coaches and team captains go about getting the job done and often with the same results whatever the approach. Sustaining motivation throughout the season is one of the coach's most difficult tasks since the team's moods, cohesion and attitudes will shift throughout the year as their form and match results fluctuate. The coach must use his own common sense, personality and all available staff and resources in a practical way to build up different individuals into a closely knit group who help each other and overcome all problems they meet. This will not be easy and will greatly tax the coach's patience, energy and perseverance, especially if things start to go wrong with individuals or the team; this is where he will have to show his ingenuity. The coach, team captain and players need to work with, not against, each other to achieve success. To be effective over a season the team needs co-operation, drive and continuous motivation between coach, team captain and the players in the squad.

The coach

He must want himself and his team to do well in the game. A 'never-say-die' attitude that gets through to his players can make them develop the same qualities and thus get the best performance out of them.

The team captain

He must also want to do well and win. If he and the coach have respect for each other and if the captain has the personality to influence the players on and off the field, then the team has a lot going for it in the psychological sense.

The players

The players, in general, must all want to be 'winners' and must be prepared to endure set-backs such as injuries, defeats and losses of form to gain eventual success.

Teams like Liverpool, Manchester United and Leeds United all have had psychologically superior teams over the past twenty years, due to a highly motivated staff and players all working towards the same objective.

Individual players' and the team's form ebbs and flows throughout the season. The team will be playing one or two matches a week for the season and will be trying to reach a peak of mental and physical performance for each match over a lot of matches and over a long period of time. It is a long time for players to maintain enthusiasm, maximum effort and motivation towards practices and matches. The coach must make sure that this does not become a problem.

Many coaches like to see their team go to the top early in the season as 'front-runners', while others are happier if their team is lying within striking distance of the leaders and the pressure is not so great on them.

Guide-lines

The position of the team in the league at any one time is important as it will guide the coach on how he motivates the team. There are three categories:

High in the table – On top or near the top and possible league winners.
Mid-table – Around half-way – relatively safe from relegation but too far away from promotion.
Near the bottom – On or near the bottom with relegation a distinct possibility.

HIGH IN THE TABLE

The coach's job is to keep up the momentum by giving the players increased coaching and fitness work. He must look out, however, for over-confidence and complacency in his players, and when he spots it he must be prepared to give players a jolt to get them concentrating again. On the other hand, certain players may start to show signs of mental and physical staleness which may be caused by the pressure from being at the top of the league or by fatigue. In such an instance, the player can be rested for a week or so away from the soccer environment or else the training programme can be varied to include less fitness work. Both of these approaches may improve the player's well-being and zest for the game again.

MID-TABLE

This is often the coach's biggest motivational problem, as the team will have no real incentives such as promotion or relegation to fight for or against. The players still want to win, but often they will find it difficult to build themselves up for the match and this feeling can be transmitted to or from the coach, thus decreasing motivation. Often, teams below them will beat them because they are more highly motivated, while they in turn will often win against teams above themselves for the same reason. The team shows occasional flashes of what it is capable of, but the sense of urgency has gone and the team begins to stagnate. The coach must re-motivate himself and place new objectives before his players, possibly even preparing for the following season by buying in new players, or experimenting by working players in new positions, or by developing different systems of play.

NEAR THE BOTTOM

Teams in this category will usually begin to develop a defeatist and negative attitude in their play which in effect means a loss of confidence. The players may go through the motions of declaring that they will win the next match, but inwardly they believe they will be beaten and, as a consequence, they play erratically from fear, afraid to take chances. By his attitude and personal example of calmness and patience with the players and their problems, the coach must remove the fear element from the situation. He must not become emotional with players, thus increasing the pressure on them (unless, of course, they are not trying); instead, he must support them and assure them that if they keep doing the things that they are good at, the situation will improve. The coach must stop players from thinking about the results and instead start them thinking about reaching individual objectives that he has set them, simplifying each person's role in the team and giving him a target for which to aim in the match. For example, 'mark a certain player from the other team', 'hit early crosses into the goal area,' or 'shoot every available chance'. After the match and at half-time the coach should focus the players' attention on the things he has given them to do — praise them when they are doing well and encourage the others who may be struggling. This will give them some success to build on.

Before the match

'In the dressing-room you've got to have that certain feeling around; however, it has only to go to a certain level because when it goes above this level it changes from inspiration to fear, when it becomes dangerous to performance, especially to younger players.' *Malcolm Allison*.

The coach must try to get the correct emotional tension level in each individual and in the team as a whole for maximum performance in the match. This is difficult to do as the coach can over-excite players or fail to see that they require stimulus, both of which will mean an erratic performance. The coach will attempt to motivate his team by a mixture of methods — emotional excitement, reason and conditioning — to get players to focus in specific ways on their own and their opponents' game in order to beat them. Individuals vary in their pre-game preparation and the process of 'getting set' starts as soon as the player starts to think about the forthcoming match, which may be weeks, days or hours before kick-off time.

The coach, when getting his team ready to meet a certain team in a match, prepares them on the basis that they will play a team that is either more successful than, on a par with, or less successful than, themselves. The preparation for each of these categories could be different. These guide-lines should be considered:

Playing a more successful team

When meeting a team like this, it is often a good idea to give the players the feeling of being 'underdog' to give them a psychological advantage. However, if they feel that due to the opponents' reputation they have no chance, then the coach must get to work to make them see that the opposition has certain weaknesses which can be exploited.

Playing a team on a par with themselves

The coach must try to gain a psychological advantage for his team by challenging his players to show that they are better without any doubt. Whichever way he can, he must gain an advantage for his team. Past results can be used to show how the games were won or lost.

Playing a less successful team

There is a danger of over-confidence here that the coach must put right. Often, no matter how coaches try to make the players see the seriousness of the situation, the players, although they seem to be preparing properly, do not prepare or train during the week with the same urgency and as a result perform badly. The players seem subconsciously to relax, thinking that they will win the game without moving into top gear, and as a consequence they are not motivated enough for the game. When they do start to realise that they have a fight on their hands, they often find that they cannot raise their motivational level enough to retrieve the game. When playing teams who are near to relegation, it is easy for the players to become complacent. This sort of thing does happen and players must understand why.

Finding the right motivational level

The degree of motivation and stimulation of a player is vital. If it is too near either end of the scale, the player's performance can be disrupted. The job of finding the correct 'mind-set' for his players is a difficult one for the coach. Players may be too high or too low for a variety of reasons, only some of which may be discovered by the coach. Factors such as confidence in his own and team's ability and the closeness and importance of the forthcoming match, can all influence the player's level of motivation for the fixture. The problem for the coach is not merely to get the player geared up for the match, but to raise or lower him to the correct level of excitement. The coach looks for signs for guidance.

Some signs to look for

The first physical signs that the player is getting ready for action is when the heart and lungs start increasing their rate and the muscle groups start to tense. Individuals will exhibit signs such as shaking or trembling of limbs, excessive sweating, toilet difficulties, ceasing to talk or talking more than usual, stomach cramp or vomiting (a few top-class players are sick fairly regularly before a match). It will be obvious that players who are not experienced, and who do not have the necessary skills, fitness and tactical understanding ingrained in their systems, will be disrupted by nervousness. For example, skills which demand fine muscular touch and rapid decisions will be very difficult, if not impossible, to reproduce in a competitive match. The coach should also remember that motivation and excitement are catching and a player or team can be affected by others or by the situation. A team that is under-motivated before a match can sometimes be aroused by a comment made by the opposition's coach, for example, that his team will annihilate their team. It must be remembered, however, that the over-excitable coach is a liability and if he cannot control his emotions he may push his team 'over the top' psychologically.

Guide-lines for finding the correct motivation level

PLAY UP OR PLAY DOWN THE IMPORTANCE OF THE MATCH

Over-excited players can often be calmed down by placing the match in its proper perspective — it is not World War III, it is only a game. The reverse procedure can be used with the player who is apathetic and does not seem to be very interested in playing. The coach can stress the importance of the match, the size of the crowd and the financial incentives, or mention whatever is likely to motivate the player.

ACCEPTING RESPONSIBILITY

The coach can take pressure off a player who is too keyed-up by speaking to him and reassuring him that provided the player tries to follow the pre-match plans set out by the coach, he has no need to worry as the coach will accept the responsibility for failure. Equally, players who are too 'low' must be made to accept responsibility for their contribution to and part in the outcome — and the enquiry to come later!

DRESSING-ROOM ATMOSPHERE

The presence of others in the dressing-room can have a disruptive effect, so only the coach and the team who are playing should be

94

present. Reserve players should be sent out and the door closed so that the coach and players can prepare effectively. Individual clubs sometimes believe in keeping the squad together as a 'family' to prepare in a ritual way for the match, while others feel that match preparation is an individual thing and players should get rid of any excess nervous tension in their own way. Some may sit quietly, while others may involve themselves in horseplay — which should be stopped if taken to extremes. As a rule, the coach, by his own example, should continually educate his players to prepare properly and remind the players that they can let their hair down after they have won, not before! Many players take the attitude of Colin Bell, the Manchester City and English International midfield player: 'Football is a serious business; some players release their nervousness through light-hearted antics and have to have the understanding of their team-mates in this. However, I cannot help becoming inwardly annoyed at this as I am more confident of the outcome of the match that day if everyone prepares quietly and seriously, with a mood of determination.'

COACH'S 'PEP TALK'

The coach can affect players' tension levels by a properly conducted pep talk. The coach should understand that each player is different and a simple direct appeal by the coach to the team is likely to affect players to a lesser or greater degree. Sometimes, the coach can bring in his team manager who may be better at motivating a certain player than he is, or the assistant coach, who may be better at calming the players down when they are too tense. The coaches can operate in this way, using their strengths to regulate the motivational level of the players.

Leeds United F.C., under the direction of late trainer Les Cocker, warm up on the field before meeting Spurs. The 'special' warm-up not only prepared them physically for the forthcoming match but helped to give them a psychological edge over their opponents.

PRE-GAME WARM-UP

The warm-up can be designed specifically to raise or lower teams' motivational levels. Players who are too tense can reduce their anxiety and tension level by the use of a good pre-game warm-up which will fire them slightly and as a result relax them. The warm-up is important physically and psychologically in preparing the players for battle, and the duration and its intensity will depend on the players' needs and the particular situation. Often, players will 'drop' or get too 'high' just before a match, due to travel problems or anxiety about the outcome of the game, and this can leave them feeling weak, tired, and sickly. The warm-up can be useful for releasing excess tension or cheering up a player in these circumstances. It can also help to alleviate players' fears before the game by getting them accustomed gradually to the playing area, crowd and atmosphere and the chance to rehearse their techniques and skills. Quite a few professional clubs have devised a sound warm-up routine, while some individual players have their own specific routine to prepare them for the match.

Psychological pressure

Players are prey to doubts and fears that put them under pressure before the match begins and which as a result inhibit their performance (e.g. fear of physical intimidation and injury, fear of facing a certain player, etc). If the player is not confident of his and his team's ability to do well against the opposition, he will begin to have anxieties which in turn will undermine his chances of success. The coach must be careful in selecting a new player for a competitive match, as putting a young and inexperienced player into the team too soon, with the result that he performs badly, can have a very damaging effect on his confidence and he will find it difficult to recover from the experience. It takes a certain kind of personality in a young player to cope with the psychological pressure of increased tempo and more physical approach in the game and more hostility from fans. The coach is responsible for preparing his players for competition and knowing when they are ready, not only in the skills, tactical and fitness sense, but also psychologically. As soon as the coach thinks the player is ready for inclusion in the team, he should prepare him gradually by increasing pressure (similar to that in the real match) until he can learn to control his emotions. Some players need longer preparation than others. The coach must be patient and adapt his approach to the player's needs, making sure that he does not lose patience and rush things. The following guide-lines will help the coach prepare his player psychologically for a match.

Get to know your player

The coach must get to know the player as quickly as he can and try to diagnose why the player is anxious or weak in a certain area. If the player is receptive and open with the coach in informal discussions, he might be able to discover what some of his problems are.

Obtain help from other sources

Often it is difficult to get through to a player who for some reason is over-anxious, and discreet enquiries can be made of the player's parents and friends which might give the coach an insight into the problem. The coach, however, must be sensitive and ethical in obtaining this information, because should the player think the coach has been going behind his back he will cease to respect him. The information can be acquired in casual conversation and often it can be most useful in helping the coach to find out what the problem might be and how best to solve it.

Look for signs

Players who are over-tense can show signs of anger when confronted with psychological pressure, especially those with limited self-control. Some players lose confidence and do not try to perform their skills in the game. They become quiet and isolated from team-mates. In others, defence mechanisms take over, and the player will blame everyone but himself for errors; or a player may become so anxious about his performance in the match that he is angry with himself or aggressive with coach and team-mates. Knowing why the player is doing these things will help the coach to understand that the player needs help in developing self-control and living with match pressure.

Therapy

The player's tensions can be lowered by the careful use of hot and cold baths or showers, massage, the playing of relaxing music, or suitable heated rooms with beds to lie on.

When the coach thinks he has identified the problem, he must find the best way of lessening or removing the circumstances that affect the player so that he can withstand and live with the psychological pressure of the match. The coach can perhaps best help by designing the practice near to the level of stress that will be encountered in the match and by conditioning the players to perform their skills and play the game well when under pressure.

Superstition

Many players have relatively harmless little superstitions such as coming out of the dressing-room last, touching a certain boot, or holding a ball. Why do they do this? Basically, they are anxious over the forthcoming match, and anxiety breeds superstition. How should the coach treat superstition? If the players have little rituals which do not seem to interfere with their performance, they should be tolerated. However, if a player is constantly changing his superstitions and blaming things such as bad luck, 'jinx teams', or something he did differently that day, the coach must get the player to accept responsibility for his own performance. He must show by his own attitude that the team should not rely on luck to win matches, but instead should focus on the real factors that win or lose matches. If they lose, players must accept that certain things went wrong – not events outside their jurisdiction, but errors that can be put right! Generally, the coach should discourage superstition by not mentioning it, for although there is an element of chance inherent in every game, the law of averages says that if you do the correct things more often than not, then you win.

A considerable number of players allow their minds to be pre-set for the remainder of the game by the outcome of the *first touch* of the ball, believing that accurate passes equal good performance and vice versa. For example, some players will give an easy first pass, an aggressive player may make sure that he stops his opposite number with the first tackle to intimidate him, or a team may channel the ball back through the team for the goalkeeper to get a touch at it in easy circumstances. By his own positive attitude, the coach can help the players to realise that this is unreasonable and that a player making a mistake in the first minute is the same as one making a mistake in the ninetieth. The warm-up should provide players with plenty of opportunity to touch the ball, thus allowing them to experience early success or make their mistakes *before* the game!

Summary:
Motivation is one of the coach's key means to success and it will greatly depend on his personality, attitude and methods of getting players interested in becoming better performers and accepting the means by which they can develop.

7

COMMUNICATION

Good communication between the team manager, coach and players is vital to the team's success. The coach spends much of his time passing on ideas and information to his players and if he fails to communicate effectively to them it will lead to confusion and frustration for everyone. The coach must remember that each player is different and his approach must differ to cater for this. For example, some players will respond to a quiet, friendly and persuasive approach while others will react better to a firm, no-nonsense set of directions.

Principles of communication

The following are three principles of good communication:

Ensure players understand the message

Often coaches think that because they have told players something, they will understand what is wanted. This is often not so, as players vary in their capacity to receive, sort out and memorise information. The coach must see that his message is fully understood by all his players. He must use simple words – and as few as possible – and he must avoid too much jargon, which may confuse players. Players who do not fully understand what has been discussed should see the coach on his own for further explanation.

The instruction must be positive

Coaches must always be hard and positive when talking to players, never depressing, defeatist or unclear about the situation. It is no use continually telling a player or team that they are doing something wrong without telling them *why* they are doing it wrong and *how* they can correct it. For example, a coach who informs a player that he has passed a 'bad ball' is not telling the player anything he does not know already; but informing him that he hit a bad pass because he passed the ball at the wrong time or to the wrong man is much more positive and helps the player to improve. This does not mean that players should not be criticised; they should, but criticism should be constructive. Ian Greaves, team manager of Wolverhampton Wanderers F.C., the English League club, once told me that you should never say to a player or team 'See how it goes' before a match as this reflects a lack of confidence in what you are doing. Coaches must be confident and stimulating in their talks to players.

The player must be involved

Two-way communication between the coach and players, where questions and ideas are passed between them is generally very productive. Encouraging players to discuss matters will add to their knowledge of the game and motivate them to improve their play. The more questions the coach can answer well, the more respect he will gain from his players; however, he must never pretend that he knows the answer to a question when he does not. It is more honest to say that you do not know and ask if any other player knows the answer. If he does, give him full credit; however, if no one knows, inform the players that you will find out from other sources as soon as possible. There is a danger in discussion that players talk too much and ask negative or illogical questions; in these circumstances the coach must instruct such players that they should communicate in a more direct manner.

Methods of communication

There are several methods of communication that the coach can employ with his players, but the methods must take into consideration such factors as the personality of the player, the reason for communicating with the player and what the aim is, the best place in the circumstances to talk to the player (e.g. the training area, the coach's office, the dressing-room).

The command

The coach must be clear and definite with his instructions and tell the player exactly what he should do. For example, he might say to a player who is giving his opponent too much room, 'I want you to get closer to the attacker and stop him turning with the ball'. This method is effective when time is short and players need quick and simple information, say at half-time, or when there is a need for urgent instruction.

The discussion

There must be effective dialogue between coach and players for efficient performance and improvement to take place. This will be enhanced through relaxed discussion where both can air their views freely. Often a player will open up more than he would in a formal team talk where the atmosphere is more inhibiting. Players who are shy or lack confidence can be helped to overcome this in two ways.
(a) *Question and answer technique*
He asks players for their ideas and suggestions on overcoming specific problems. This stimulates the player to think and communicate.

(b) *Challenging players*

Another technique is to challenge the players to find answers to problems. For example, 'Let's see if you can break this packed defence down' or 'There's no way that you can score more goals from that restart – is there?'

The coach must ensure that the discussion does not stray too far from its original objective.

Team talk

The team talk is where more serious and immediate matters are relayed to the players by the coach in a one-way system without much interruption. The team talk can cover anything from team discipline to tactical preparation for a forthcoming match. The tone of the voice and talk should vary according to the needs of the moment and the coach's objective.

Match analysis technique

The coach can fire factual and objective information at players by analysing and communicating details about their performance. This must be handled carefully as it might tend to threaten some players if they take it as a personal criticism. The coach must persuade and assure his players that it is being done to improve individual and team performance. He should analyse parts (midfield or back four) involving a larger number of players where faults can be shown clearly to the team without individuals being identified and where they can see what needs improving without being shown up in front of their team-mates. If a coach wants to show an individual player some fault, he must do so privately.

Visual technique

The coach can communicate information and ideas with visual aids and demonstration. This can be done in a variety of ways. A bright and well-designed notice-board can be the focal point in the dressing-room and can communicate up-to-date information such as training schedules, match reports, travel arrangements for away matches, and team meetings. Films or video tapes of matches played can also be valuable in letting players see the good or bad parts of their performance. The coach can also communicate ideas by setting up demonstrations for players to see and discuss items from it. This is discussed more fully in the chapter entitled **Soccer Skill Learning**.

Match communication

It is important that players give each other reliable information quickly during the match. This can help the play and team organisation. Often the goal-keeper or players at the back are better situated to see what is

happening and thus able to call to a team-mate to take appropriate
action. A considerable number of goals are given away because one or
more defenders fail to communicate properly. How many times do we
see an attacker sneaking in to score a goal while defenders argue about
who should mark an attacker to prevent him scoring? The coach must
spend some time during practice in ensuring that all players are familiar
with the terms to use when calling to each other, and that they call
clearly, at the correct time and in a positive, constructive way.
Pre-arranged signals can be used at restarts to indicate which routine
will be used by the players. ·

Getting the message over

Effective speaking

A coach's job requires him to communicate verbally with players,
other staff members, and often the media. Some coaches, although good
at talking to players in their own environment of the dressing-room and
playing-field, do not come over well to the media. They could improve
their powers of communication by critical analysis of their speech,
choice of words and the style and delivery used. Sir Alf Ramsey, the
ex-England International Team Manager, undertook speech training to
improve his power of communication.

How to speak is important in your relationship with players. Accents
are usually all right; however, words affect the way players react, so the
coach needs to give thought to his vocabulary. How the coach feels
about coaching will be reflected by how he speaks about it (e.g. cynical
coaches will speak negatively). Speech should be simple, logical and
clear; the coach should use few words and use terms which are
meaningful to the players. Positive instructions must be given which
inspire players to want to improve – the coach should avoid negative
statements such as 'bad pass'. Indeed, a player must be told why he
made a bad pass and how he can make a good one. Use the voice for
effect. For example, talk quickly to show enthusiasm, low in an
emotional way to 'fire up' the team for a match, or loudly to emphasise.
Repeat important statements to emphasise them but avoid bad habits in
speech. Talk directly to the players or squad by looking at them and
opening your mouth wide as you speak.

The communication environment

Players will be less receptive to your talk with them if the
circumstances are wrong. Often coaches will talk to players on the
training area or pitch after they have been involved in a hard physical
session, when they are fatigued, both mentally and physically; or else
they will try to gain players' attention when they are sitting down and
cooling off after sweating. Talking to players in these situations, or above
the noise in the dressing-room, is a waste of breath. The coach should
wait until the players have showered and cooled down, or at least until
they are in a reasonably receptive state.

Ron Greenwood, the former England Team Manager, talks with Laurie Cunningham, the Real Madrid and England winger, during a training session. Communicating in a one-to-one situation can be very profitable since the player and Team Manager are given each other's undivided attention, and the opportunity to listen and express their separate viewpoints.

Position relative to players

The coach must ensure that he stands where every player can *see* and *hear* him clearly, with the wind at his back if talking to the players in the open so that his voice will carry to them. It is a good idea to try to make sure that the sun is not shining directly into the players' or his own eyes; this can be very distracting.

The media

Press, radio and television can be very useful for promoting the players and club. But there are also dangers involved, as some reporters seem to be more interested in the sensational issues rather than the routine ones involving the everyday running of the club. The coach must be careful when making statements to the Press, particularly after a poor team display when he may be angry, lest he says something that he regrets later. He should try to build up a rapport with the local media and co-operate as far as possible with their representatives, because not only can the coach communicate current information about the team to the public, but he can also help his players by editing match reports, and after-match statements. This can indirectly communicate his ideas and give praise or criticism to individual team members. Statements made by the coach after the game should be carefully thought out and worded to avoid any misunderstandings. As a general rule he must avoid criticising individual players in public — he could talk about general play or even units of the team, but to talk about a player in public could alienate him permanently. It is far better to see a player on his own on the Monday morning to discuss his performance. Another golden rule is never to criticise in public a player or team that you are soon to meet as it will probably motivate them to try that much harder against your own team! When talking to pressmen before a match, continental coaches are masters of playing down their team's chances. This is psychologically sound, as it helps give the opposition a false sense of security and thus takes some pressure away from his own team.

The coach can write a match report in the local Press or for radio which can convey such things as concern about, satisfaction with, anger at, and support for the team's display and current form. This can be an important medium for communicating with the players, at any level — from schoolboy to top professional.

NORMAN HUNTER

I am sure that the signings of Alan Birch and Jimmy Mann on Monday will give the place a lift, and get things moving again.

Something needed to be done, because we have been faltering a little in recent weeks, and I was delighted to be able to bring these two players to Oakwell.

Ideally I would still like to sign another striker to strengthen the squad further, but, like all other clubs these days, we are governed by what money is available to us.

Meanwhile, Alan is due to make his debut for us tonight and I trust that you will give him your usual warm Oakwell welcome.

Tonight's game is, in fact, the start of a very important period, for we have five of our next six fixtures here at Oakwell, and it is imperative that we put them to the best possible advantage if we are to continue our promotion challenge.

It is totally, utterly up to us. The ball is in our court. The opportunity is there for us to make a strong claim for a place in the First Division, and we can blame no-one but ourselves if we fail.

There will, of course, have to be a great deal of improvement on our performance at Cardiff on Saturday. I would put that down as our worst of the season. It was a good point, but a most disappointing game to watch.

And if you analyse it, we have dropped points we should have won against teams in the bottom six or seven in the table, and we must put a stop to that.

We have gone part way towards it by tightening up defensively, but it seems that by doing so we have lost out at the other end, where goals are becoming much rarer. We need to strike a happy balance, and I believe that Alan Birch will help us do that.

Despite recent comparatively disappointing form when measured against earlier performances, we are still very much in there with a shout as far as promotion is concerned.

Team Managers Norman Hunter (Barnsley F.C.) and Roy McFarland (Bradford City F.C.) communicated ideas via the Club programme and local newspaper.

Improving communication

Get to know your players

Coaches must not treat players merely as units in the team. They should get to know each player as a person by finding out as much background information as possible — information that directly or indirectly affects the player's performance and potential. This may include the player's relationship with his parents and family, his objectives in life and in the game, his school and academic work, his heroes, his general likes and dislikes and his interests. The coach must not interrogate the player; any talk of this kind should be in a relaxed atmosphere, for example when a player is giving his background details for filling in a form. The idea is to get a general understanding of the player and the environment from which he comes. A player who comes from a deprived background is likely to have a different approach and objectives from a player who has come from a secure one. All information gained in this way must be kept completely confidential by the coach, otherwise he may lose the player's trust.

Face-to-face conversations

Often the coach does not have a lot of time; but, where he can, he should have chats with individual or groups of players at every opportunity. For example, these may be private interviews or discussions in the office, encounters in the corridor or dressing-room, or talking to players in the club coach travelling to and from a match. These 'give and take' talks present an excellent opportunity for exchanging confidences and can help to build trust between the coach and the player. It is very important that, even when angry at the player's attitude and behaviour, the coach *never* uses this information against the player, otherwise word will get round the team that he repeats things which have been said to him in confidence.

Players' committee

Some soccer clubs have a small committee of players selected by the squad to represent their interests. The team captain should be on it and matters such as the training programme, tactics, and club rules can be discussed. The areas which cannot be discussed, i.e. Board policy or finances, may be areas in which the coach feels the players should not be involved and players should be aware of this from the start. It can enhance communication as each player feels that, through his committee, his voice is being heard, and it can give the coach valuable feedback about the current feelings of the team on a variety of topics. It should be conveyed to the committee that although the meetings should give them a chance to air their opinions, it should not become a grumbling session; instead, the whole atmosphere should be constructive.

Listening to players

For coaches to become good communicators, they must learn to become good listeners. Failing to listen to players will lose the coach many chances to build up trust and learn about individuals. He should listen to what the player is saying without being impatient and interrupting – and should then demonstrate that he has understood. He will gain players' respect in this way and assist better communication.

Communication will be enhanced if the coach has an 'open-door' policy, the players feel free to talk to him confidentially at any time about any subject that may be bothering them. A coach cannot expect commitment from a player on the coach's ideas if the coach has no time to listen to him.

'Body language' feedback

The coach can learn to 'read' players just as he has learnt to read the game, by becoming aware of and understanding how they are reacting and feeling about club matters. The problem is that a player may *say* that everything is all right, disguising his real feeling that everything is all wrong. In this case, the coach can learn a lot by identifying and interpreting body signals which will give him information about the player's present state of mind. Some coaches are very intuitive and can read signs naturally, but all coaches can become better at this with practice. For example, the face can give away fear, surprise, joy and anger, and players can show negative reactions to the coach's words by frowning and narrowing the eyes, or stifling a yawn, or by showing no facial reaction at all. A player may turn away from the coach and avoid looking at him as he speaks or he may sit hunched tensely in a chair. There is a considerable amount of literature available on the science of 'body language' which can help the coach to understand more about the attitude of players.

All too often there is a difference between what coaches *think* they have said to players and what they have *actually* said, and between how they feel they have approached the situation and how the player feels he has been treated. Often, a misunderstanding gets between the intended and the actual action and results in a barrier between coach and player; usually temporary and easily resolved, but sometimes permanent. In a sport such as soccer it is inevitable that communication problems will arise. For example, instructions may have been unrealistic or were not heard properly in the excitement of the dressing-room before a match; a highly-sensitive player may take offence at a particular remark, or a player or coach's attitude may be coloured by prejudice, jealousy or frustration. The coach must be aware that certain words and the emotional way in which they are used have a strong influence on certain players and virtually none on others. The coach must consider what he says, and how he says it, as even the most innocent speech can sometimes be misunderstood. This is because players may have been conditioned in the use of certain words or phrases which make them feel degraded, angry, ridiculed or frightened. Claudio Coutinho, the ex-coach to the Brazilian International soccer team, mentioned the fact that he has been surprised a few times by the unusual reactions of some of his players during his pre-match pep talks which were intended to stimulate the team. For example, when using the phrase 'We must exert ourselves to the full because of the occasion', some players had a positive reaction increasing the will to win, others showed no reaction at all, and felt depressed and crushed by the responsibility of representing their country and perhaps giving a poor performance.

Team talks

The coach spends a lot of time speaking to his players in both a formal and informal way. The match cycle illustrated opposite shows the effort made.

Tactical talk

This is best done at least two hours before the match, when the players are still fairly receptive (unlike immediately before the match when excitement and tension is high). Usually the opponent's strengths and possible weaknesses are analysed and assessed as individuals and as a team. Players should be encouraged to ask and discuss anything that is not clear to them – the coach should make sure that each player

The Communication Cycle

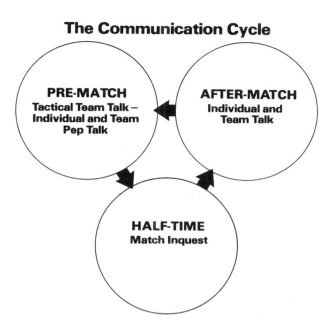

fully understands his role in the team and exactly what his responsibilities are in the match. Any points of disagreement have to be sorted out now. It is better if some scouting of the opposition has been done beforehand, as it gives players confidence to know what they are likely to be facing. However, the coach must be careful how he presents the information on the opposition; he should not make them appear unbeatable! He ought to reassure the team that if they perform their roles correctly and stick to the team plan, they have nothing to fear and stand a good chance of winning. The tactical talk should not last too long and it should be clear and simple. It is hard for players to concentrate effectively for longer than forty minutes.

Pre-match pep talk

This is often badly done by coaches, mainly through lack of thought or conviction. To be effective the pep talk must be fresh and inspirational, and the approach must be changed when needed. A lot of coaches give repetitive pep talks week after week and try to cram in a lot of last-minute information. This is wrong as players are under a lot of pressure at this time and are unreceptive to all but the simplest information. The pep talk is essentially a last-minute 'stimulator' to encourage players to do their best in the match. It is often best given in an emotional way as this is usually what inspires players at this stage. The coach must decide whether the players are too 'high' or 'low' and temper his pep talk accordingly. Some players will need calming down, while others will need boosting. The pep talk must cater for individuals as well as the team. It is best to sit down beside the player as he is getting changed and talk quickly and quietly to him about the key points.

Some coaches feel a bit uncomfortable about approaching their players before a match, but they have no reason to be – players expect it as it supports them. The coach should *never* mention a player's weaknesses before the game as it is likely to lower his confidence. He should talk positively about his strengths and how well he is going to do. For example, if a player is a good dribbler, the coach should tell him so and tell him to take on defenders. Coaches are often anxious about the outcome of a game and transmit their anxiety to the players by their talk and manner. For example, if the coach says 'Make sure you don't take chances in the goal area', often players will 'drop' or go too 'high' psychologically. While travelling to a match, some players may feel weak, sick or generally look unwell. The coach must never say to a player 'You look terrible' or ask, 'Are you all right?', (even if they feel like saying it), as it may depress the player still further – and make raising his morale more difficult. He should not allow any outsider into the dressing-room during his pre-match pep talk as this could be inhibiting. The coach should lock the door to all but his immediate staff and the eleven players named for the match.

Half-time talk

This talk by coaches or managers is a mixture of tactical direction and stimulus. During this period the coach must get the players' full attention. He should try to get through to the players who present a possible threat to the team performance and support them as the situation demands. The more reliable performers generally do not need this, so time can be spent on the others. The coach must keep control of his emotions. He must use every minute effectively by getting directly to the point. He must think clearly and objectively about what is going wrong with the individuals and team, and what he is going to say and do to put it right. The coach should never let his anger and disappointment influence his analysis and objectivity. He must make the players listen and make sure his points get across to them. The worst mistake is to tell a team they are doing well at half-time! They will often consciously or subconsciously relax – he must try to find them a new target to aim for. There are two games, not one – one in each half. They have played one game, now it is a new one. Talks at half-time include predictions of what the coach thinks will happen in the second half, based largely on what has happened in the first half, but players must be prepared to be able to adapt their tactics on the field should the predictions prove false.

Match inquest

Some coaches take their anger out on players after a game by locking dressing-room doors and subjecting the team to abuse or anger after the team has performed poorly. The dressing-room is a potentially explosive place after a defeat and the coach is usually in a better position to speak to players when he and the players have had time to cool off!

Players and coach are still under a certain amount of emotional pressure after the excitement of a match, whatever the result. If the team has done well they should be congratulated but not excessively so. A coach must remember that his preparation for the next match is beginning and the players must keep their feet on the ground. He should not criticise players or team until they have cooled down. Players must be approached, if at all, depending on their personality and how they have played – if they have played badly they are likely to be on their guard. If they are cocky and have played well, they should be told they have done 'all right', and players who have tried hard but had a poor game should be supported. Occasionally, when the team has played very badly because of lack of effort and a poor attitude, then the coach can 'have a go' verbally immediately after the match. This can be done for two reasons – it can release anger from the coach and it can let the players know in no uncertain terms that things will have to change.

The match inquest is therefore best done a few days after the match – usually before the first training session and after players have had the weekend to relax and think about their personal performance and contribution to the result.

Blocks to communication

Often the coach will think he is communicating with his players when in fact he is not. These blocks are sometimes difficult to spot: the following guide-lines will help the coach:

Question players

The coach can interrupt his talk and ask players at random, or the ones he thinks are not paying attention, to repeat what he has been talking about. The coach must be subtle and see that he does not let players feel that they are being ridiculed. For example, he might say to a player, 'Well, Ian, what do you think of that idea?' If the player cannot answer satisfactorily the coach can use a 'questioning' facial expression to let the group know that they must concentrate on the information going out to them; the player is reminded to listen.

Signs from players

The coach can learn much from looking at players' movements and manner when talking to them as everyone exhibits general and specific peculiarities. Players who are non-cooperative can display signs such as standing a longer distance than normal from the coach or moving away as he is talking. Often players show 'defensive' signs such as crossing their arms in front of their chests, looking away from the coach as he speaks, yawning, drawing an imaginary line with their feet between themselves and the coach as he is speaking, shuffling their feet and refusing to speak or get involved in conversation even when the coach tries hard to start a discussion going. Sometimes the players will be unable to look at the coach directly as he speaks. Signs like these can be interpreted easily by the coach and clearly he must change his talk to regain attention.

Illogical speaking

Coaches must ensure that they present their information logically, taking the players gradually through the various stages so they understand the topic fully before moving on to more difficult areas. Some coaches jump from one area to another, but they should be logical and orderly so that the theme can be developed properly.

Bad speaking habits

Some coaches have certain peculiarities which block effective communication, such as repeating themselves over and over again, using phrases such as 'you know', mumbling, or turning away from players as they speak to them. Other bad habits are putting their hands up near their mouth when speaking, or talking too quickly. The coach must look at players and speak directly to them in a simple and clear fashion.

Talking too much

Almost all coaches at some time or other are guilty of this. They should not use too many words and the ones they use should be simple and easily understood. A coach must get to the heart of the matter and stick to the point.

Summary:
The coach is often heavily involved with his players and so he will be communicating with them at individual and team level in a variety of ways. He must seek to improve his own communication ability to the fullest extent by paying attention to the established principles of good communication.

8

TEAM SPIRIT

Most successful teams have team spirit in abundance. All team managers try to achieve co-operation between individuals but are often disappointed by a player's or team's response. Building up and maintaining team spirit is a very difficult task for the team manager as players differ in their degree of responsibility to the team. Some are selfish, only wanting to do things that make themselves look good.

The team's level of success will rise and fall throughout the season and at some time the team will hit a losing streak, with injuries and problems within the club. This tests the loyalties, patience and responsibility of coach and players to the limit, and this is where team spirit is most important. In situations like this it is easy to blame something or someone else for individual failure and the team manager must realise that there can be a lot of hidden disharmony in the team. For example, there is likely to be rivalry between two or more players for positions in the team, personality clashes between team manager, coach and/or other players, and jealousy of the so-called 'star' player in the team. The problem for the team manager is to get the players working with, not against, each other, for as long as it takes success to come.

The team manager must consider the following factors when trying to build up team spirit at the club.

The attitude of the staff

The team manager, coach and staff will all have a profound effect on the team spirit at the club. The team manager must accept full responsibility for the team image and conduct, whether positive or negative. A team which consistently involves itself in foul and vicious play, or has unsporting attitudes, must have a team manager who either has not the strength of character to control the players or turns a blind eye to their conduct as long as they keep winning (or may even encourage rough play as a team policy). It would be in the interests of soccer if team managers in the first category would obtain a tough coach to implement the favourable image that he personally would like to create but cannot. In the other two categories, one hopes to change the thinking of such team managers if at all possible, but if not, they must be shown up for what they are in the hope that they will be forced out of the game. The team manager must have the moral courage to stand up for his principles, and take full responsibility for his team's image and conduct. The staff team must work to develop respect from players by their dealings with them and also encourage respect between players for each other. This is not easy, as it will involve players and staff showing more tolerance of aspects of human behaviour that they do not like, but it is important; players who do not get on well socially are likely to carry their resentments on to the field of play and team spirit suffers as a consequence. It is unrealistic to expect all players to adjust to each other's personalities and behaviour in the same way; however, serious team problems can be minimised by the staff team. The staff must get the co-operation of other team members to help problem players readjust themselves to the team. The team manager can gain the help of the other players in being tolerant of a player's excesses of behaviour by pointing out to them that the player can be rehabilitated and become an asset to the team.

Team spirit can also be developed by organising tours or similar events where the players are brought together, and new friendships can be formed. The team manager can put certain players in the same room or arrange small competitions or events where players need to work together to win. Tony Toms, the trainer at Sheffield Wednesday F.C. and an ex-Army Commando, took the squads of players at several clubs he was with on survival courses in winter. Players went on bleak moors in snow and freezing temperatures with only a tent to protect them from the elements and very little food. The idea of such courses is to develop a sense of comradeship and team spirit in adverse conditions in the hope that this will carry through to the competitive match.

The team captain

The team captain can do much to influence team spirit and for this reason it is important to select a player who is a natural leader. During

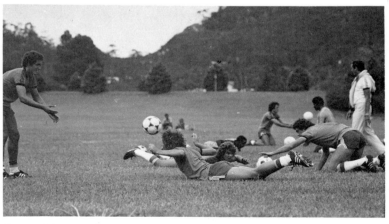

Team spirit can be forged in the training and coaching programme. Brazilian International players work together as a squad on fitness exercises in preparation for the 1978 World Cup at a Camp.

the season, various types of potential team captains will emerge – for example, the player who leads by personal example, the one who inspires by his verbal exhortations and 'presence', or the one who is the 'general' or 'playmaker' and who dictates the game by directing and persuading the other players. The team captain has responsibilities off the field as well as on it and should work in harmony with the team manager and coach to keep things running smoothly. The team captain's responsibilities will usually include:

★ Helping to create team spirit
★ Representing the team manager and coach to the team
★ Representing the team to the team manager and coach
★ Taking responsibility for tactical changes or decisions which he deems necessary during the match
★ Helping with training sessions or match analysis when required.

Problem players

Many players fail to realise that their success or failure depends on the team performance. Some players are selfish and cannot see beyond their own performance, while others play safe and will not take risks, which might mean that they are less than effective and do not help their team-mates when they should. There are different types of problem players who can cause disharmony in the dressing-room or on the field by their complete indifference to the team manager, team tactics, training and coaching programme, club rules, conduct and manners. Often it is the most talented individuals who cause problems by their unreasonbable and un-cooperative behaviour. Problem players can have a very negative effect on team spirit and the team manager must be strong in identifying them and either changing their ways or allowing them to leave the club.

Often problems occur with players who are currently out of favour with the first team and feel that they are being neglected or unjustly treated. Sometimes players who have never caused problems when in the first team show a change in attitude when dropped into the reserve team. They cause disruption by lack of effort in training, by forming cliques with other players in a similar situation and spreading rumours designed to cause dissension among the other team members. The players out of favour hope fervently that the first team are beaten, and I have heard a group of players from a professional league club cheer loudly when the opposition scored against their club. It is natural to feel dissatisfied and angry at being left out of the team. If players did not feel this their motives and commitment would be in question. However, nothing is gained by wishing failure on team-mates. The only way that anyone can be guaranteed a regular first team place is by developing a positive attitude and by regaining confidence in the reserve team and during the coaching sessions, and playing so well that the team manager must put the player back in the first team as soon as a suitable position arises.

Team 'type'

Although individuals differ in their psychological make-up, there is within the mix a team type which comes through. There are two basic types:

TYPE A
This type has strong needs for friendship and co-operation among its players even to the exclusion of the need for winning. Players will not get over-upset about losing and will tend to support each other when they do.

TYPE B
This type is mainly concerned with winning and success. The players are not worried about forming relationships but about functioning well as a team to win matches. Professional clubs are usually more inclined to this type, but not always.

The team manager would do himself a favour by ascertaining as quickly as possible which type his team tends to be and approaching them on that basis. Individuals differ in their psychological needs, such as self-esteem, being liked and respected by team-mates, and feeling part of the working team. Players practise and play together regularly and although they see much of each other they may not be concerned about friendships on and off the field. As players age, they experience varying situations with the team which may bring them to heights of ecstasy with superb team performances or to the depth of despair with inept displays. As the season goes on the team spirit will change, depending on the team's experiences which will tend to 'up' or 'down' team spirit. The team manager must find out where the team want to go, how hard they are prepared to work and what price they are prepared to pay to achieve success.

Club and team image

The club image is important to the team spirit as it can affect it in a number of ways. Outsiders can see the club and team image differently from the staff and players inside the club. Teams are seen as being well-organised, aggressive, skilful, fit and athletic, or undisciplined, inconsistent or unbalanced. The image can be positive or negative, and the team manager must ensure that if it is the first category, he builds on this to help the team spirit. If it is the second, he must work to develop a new image so that the players have confidence, belief and meaning in their part in the team, their team-mates, the team manager, coach and staff. The team manager must see that the club image is positive, while the coach must see that all individual players work hard to maintain this over a long period. One serious error by a player at the wrong time can destroy or seriously damage the image. Leeds United F.C. under Don Revie had built up an image which earned them a 'dirty' tag from critics and a suspended £3000 fine from the Football Association for persistent brushes with referees. Don Revie decided that his club and team image needed changing, so he arranged a pre-season staff and players' conference to inform them of his decision to change the team image. In practice matches, the staff coaches, acting as referees, gave deliberate wrong decisions to provoke players. At first they reacted as they had done in the past – by arguing and showing dissent – but gradually, through players being sent off from practice matches, higher club fines for players getting into trouble on the pitch, and constantly reminding them that they must show greater self-discipline, accept decisions immediately and get on with the game, the team started to improve their image.

Changing the team attitude and image

If the team's image is a negative one the coach must first seek to change the players' attitudes which are often likely to conform to this image. It is much more difficult to change an individual's attitude than it is to change the team image, as it involves the individual player more closely and means the coach must show more patience and determination. The interaction between the coach and player, and how different the desired team image is from the player's attitude, will determine what approach the coach should adopt with the individual player. It is important that when attempting to change the team's image, the coach remembers that to do this he requires the individual player's co-operation. The coach must consider these factors when trying to change a player's attitude.

DEVELOP RELATIONSHIPS

The coach must try to have informal, separate meetings with each player so that he can get to know something about him and what things are important to him, whether it is his wife and family, girlfriend, education, ambitions or hobbies. If the coach is genuine in his desire to develop better relationships, the player will feel he can trust him and will co-operate with his plans for the team. However, if a player does not wish to discuss matters outside the game of soccer then his wishes should be respected.

BUILD UP CONFIDENCE

Many players lack confidence in themselves or in the team, and the coach must do everything in his power to correct this situation. He can continually praise and encourage players who are making a real effort to change their attitude, and can spend more time on the practice area and in conversation with certain players on an individual basis in order to support them and make them feel more confident. Players should be encouraged to give their own opinions on what is needed to improve the team image and the coach should try to incorporate these in his plans where possible. A player must feel that he is a good player and the coach has a very important role to play in building up the player's self-confidence.

SET OBJECTIVES

Trouble starts at a club when the players have too much time on their hands and when they feel that the playing, as well as the training and coaching, programmes are aimless. The team manager will do much to improve team spirit if he sets realistic objectives for individual players, groups and team over the short and longer term. Things such as fitness, skills, tactics, goals for and against, behaviour, number of matches played can be set to challenge the players and team and give them something to work for together during the season.

TRAINING AND COACHING PROGRAMME

The programme can be changed by increased or reduced emphasis on fitness as opposed to on skills or tactics or vice versa, or by changing the methods. The programme must fit in with the new image (e.g. if the team manager wants a more athletic and workmanlike team, he may involve the team in a greater emphasis on running, endurance and general conditioning).

TACTICAL APPROACH

The team manager can set out to change the team image by altering the tactical approach. For example, he may feel that the approach has been too restricted and limited and does not fit in with the team's strengths. He may decide to change from an approach that has been good to look at but has not won games, to a more disciplined approach where the team do not leave themselves so vulnerable and therefore win more matches.

Changing the club image

The team manager can inject a fresh image into an old-fashioned or drab club by introducing a series of changes such as repainting the ground, having new strips, blazer or ties, new stationery, advertising slogans or club name. A symbol can be designed and reproduced on letter headings, shirts, tracksuits or blazers to promote the feeling of unity and of going places. For example, Liverpool F.C. is instantly recognisable by the Liver bird crest while Tottenham Hotspur F.C. is well known as 'the Cockerels'. The team manager must ensure that before any changes affecting the club image are introduced he has a meeting with the committee, staff and players to get their backing. Everyone must believe in what they are doing for it to have full effect. The team manager must communicate clearly to the players, staff and supporters, plus any other persons connected with the club, what he is trying to do for the club image, by meetings, newsletters, or via the local Press. Once the initial impetus has died down, the team manager must emphasise and re-emphasise the need for the new image. This can be done in a

The Italian team celebrate their World Cup triumph over West Germany in Spain. The Italian's refusal to cooperate with their own press, whom they perceived as hostile towards them, seemed to improve their motivation and teamwork.

variety of ways (e.g. meetings, informal discussions or reprimands for violation of the image) and also by praise when players show development and improvement in their attitude.

Team rules and discipline

To be successful, team members need to be self-disciplined as individuals and as a team. For example, there are players who are always getting into trouble with referees, or are regularly late for training sessions or abuse their health by late nights or other excesses. A team which tends to be complacent when meeting a team lower in the league table, or which takes irresponsible risks such as rear defenders dribbling or interpassing in tight situations around their own penalty area, is placing the success of the team at risk. All players differ in their levels of self-discipline and responsibility to the team; some are conscientious, some lack consistency in their behaviour, some are over-sensitive, while others do not seem to feel any concern for the team at all. Some team managers draw up a set of rules and disciplinary procedures to which each team member is subject regardless of the circumstances. I feel this is fraught with danger and could disrupt team spirit because some players will feel that they have been unjustly treated. Each player needs

120

to be treated as an individual and each situation on its merit. To punish with a heavy fine a player who has come late for a training session for the first time, or to give two players an equal punishment for a similar offence, when it is one player's first offence and the other has committed several, is asking for trouble. The type of team will determine what kind of rules and discipline will be required to achieve success and maintain team spirit. The team manager must make it clear to all players in the team that to be effective they need to agree on a club strategy and plan which will give them the best chance of success and that players who blatantly break the rules will be treated severely. The team manager, however, must realise that soccer is an emotional game where players will experience feelings of despair, depression, excitement, elation and lack of confidence. Most players, at some time or another, will go overboard, if only temporarily, in their reactions to situations. The team manager must be careful not to over-react when this happens; players are human, and although the player may clearly have disregarded the rules and should be disciplined, the severity of the punishment should take into consideration whether or not the player has been making a determined effort to conform to the team image and code of practice. When drawing up the team rules, the team manager must decide on the 'type' of team that he is handling and act accordingly. For example if the team tends to be disciplined and co-operative, there would be less need for rules, while if players were argumentative and selfish by nature, the disciplinary system would need to be tighter.

The team manager needs to consider the following different situations.

Competitive play

The players need to be informed clearly what is and what is not allowed on the field of play. Some players get involved in personal vendettas with opposing players. This type of player is a liability to his team as he cannot concentrate properly on the game. Other players often get into trouble with referees by 'back-chatting' to them after decisions have gone against them or by losing their self-control when intimidated, physically or verbally, by opponents. Such players put themselves and the team under psychological pressure by giving away free-kicks in dangerous positions, by cautions or by risking being sent off.

Training and coaching sessions

Players must be made to realise that the training and coaching sessions are vital to the team's success and it is the players' duty to attend. There is not much time, especially with amateur clubs, for a lot of practice, particularly in winter when daylight hours are short, so what time there is needs to be spent productively. The atmosphere of the practice sessions also sets the tone for the forthcoming competitive match and poor practice can form bad habits which come out during the match.

Personal responsibility

The team manager must make it clear that each player is responsible for his own health and level of physical fitness. Some players lack the will-power to keep themselves in shape for the competitive matches plus the many coaching and training sessions over a long season. Players in this category must be helped by whatever means the team manager has at his disposal. The coach should have some objective measures of each player's physical fitness and health problems, such as asthma, suspect knee, migraine, and weight. He should test players pre-season and during the season so that the team manager can show the results to players who are not as fit as they ought to be and try to find out the reasons for this. Some players' lifestyles may mean that they have inadequate sleep or an unsuitable diet, they smoke and drink too much or do not get enough relaxation. Obviously, a team manager cannot dictate his players' lifestyle, but if it is interfering with their playing performance they are letting the team down and the coach or team manager has every right to take steps to rectify the situation. Some players find it difficult to keep their weight down to a reasonable level in order to be at their peak of fitness and need encouragement by the team manager to do so; overweight players can have fines imposed on them. Regular fitness and health tests by the team manager will help the player to discipline himself and keep at his peak condition.

Relationships with and conduct towards staff and other players

The player must show reasonable conduct towards staff and team-mates. Obviously, in the competitive atmosphere of a soccer club relationships will suffer at times. No matter how frustrated or angry players become, the team manager must make each one aware of the need for good conduct. Allowances must be made by the team manager for occasional arguments and outbursts, but limits for such conduct must be set and players who overstep the mark must be disciplined.

The team manager is solely responsible for formulating the team rules and seeing that they are kept. He should consider the following points before deciding on them:

FEW RULES

It is wise not to have too many rules otherwise players will begin to feel that they are being stepped on for every little thing. By having too many rules the team manager makes things difficult for himself because it will be impossible to enforce them all.

FAIR RULES

The team manager must see that he sets fair rules which are seen by players to be reasonable and which are not based on his personal prejudices. Many team managers and coaches today find it difficult to adjust to the changes of attitude that have taken place in soccer and sport in general. Possible flashpoints are long hair, headbands, no shinguards, foul language and smoking in the dressing-room. The team manager must look for a second opinion from his coach and staff to ensure that his rules are not unfair or prejudiced, but he has the ultimate responsibility.

PUNISHMENT PROCEDURE

Normally, it is best to deal with problems involving punishment as soon as they appear but occasionally a tough-minded player who is a consistent offender should be kept waiting for some time to 'sweat it out' to bring home to him the gravity of the situation. The idea of punishment is not to exact revenge for misdemeanours but rather to help the player to change his conduct for his own and the team's good, and much care is necessary when taking decisions on punishment.

CLEAR COMMUNICATION

The team manager should hold a pre-season conference at which he can inform the team of the club and team rules and the disciplinary procedure for infringements of the rules. Often, angry players will come to the team manager and argue that they did not know about a certain rule or the resultant punishment. To safeguard himself, and to make sure the rules and disciplinary procedure are known to all players, the team manager, after holding the pre-season conference, should have the rules, with punishments where necessary, pinned on the dressing-room notice-board or in the players' handbook.

PLAYERS' COMMITTEE

Some professional league clubs have a small players' committee with usually the team captain and some senior or authoritative members in the group. The players' committee, with the right players, team manager and good club atmosphere, can aid team spirit, but with an easy-going team manager it can produce authority problems.

Disciplinary methods

Players can be disciplined for such things as bad conduct on the field of play, lateness, failing to turn up for training sessions or matches without good reason, lack of effort at training sessions or foul language.

The methods will of course depend on the severity of the offence and how it will affect team spirit.

Verbal Confrontation

Often all a player requires is a firm reminder of his obligations to the team given in a talk in the more 'awesome' surroundings of the team manager's office. When a player has really gone far beyond the limits of acceptable behaviour, the proverbial 'tongue lashing', done correctly, can be most effective. Some players who constantly make trouble for themselves and the team by their behaviour can sometimes be confronted angrily by the team manager with good effect. Other players may have developed negative attitudes because they have 'got away with murder' in the past and a sudden jolt from the boss, who lets him know in no uncertain terms what he expects from him in the future, can change his attitude. The verbal confrontation, however, is fraught with danger and should be considered carefully beforehand.

Fines

Monetary fines can be imposed on players for lateness, misconduct on the field of play, severe arguments or squabbles with fellow players. The amount will depend on the nature of the offence. This can be quite effective so long as the sums are set at the correct level; neither so excessive as to cause hardship nor so low as to be ineffectual. The idea of hitting players where it hurts — is probably more effective in the professional or semi-professional game.

Suspension

Players who break club rules can be suspended for a period during which they are not allowed to play in competitive matches, train with the team, or even come to the ground. The isolation of the player, especially if the team hits a winning run, can have a salutary effect on him. The length of suspension will depend on the offence. Many team managers dislike this method of disciplining as it deprives them of a good player at a time when they could do with him! However, the team manager must decide whether this method will prove to be the most effective in the long term.

Dropping a player

As has been mentioned earlier, many team managers dislike any method which deprives them of a player for a game, but in certain cases it has proved to be the necessary jolt which players needed to get them out of a complacent attitude and into a more enthusiastic frame of mind. There is a danger, however, that if a player is dropped for disciplinary reasons and the team suffers a bad defeat, the player may feel that the team cannot do without him, especially if he plays in the next match and the team wins. This course of action should be treated with caution.

Extra training

Players who cause problems and fail to work anywhere near their maximum can be put through the mill with extra physical training of a sufficiently hard and unpleasant nature to deter them from risking a repeat performance. The team manager does not mention it, but the players suddenly notice that the tempo and quantity of the session has changed. This has a limited role to play, especially with more experienced players.

Isolation

Some team managers use an 'avoidance' method with players who persistently break the rules, and isolate them to the point where they are ignored completely by the coach. If the team manager is respected by the player and he lifts the boycott when his attitude improves it can be very effective. Generally this method should only be used very occasionally when other methods have proved ineffective.

Brian Clough, the Nottingham Forest Team Manager, believes in a strict disciplinary code for his players which has helped to create good team spirit and has brought success to his club.

Disciplinary procedure

The team manager must face disciplinary team problems as soon and as fairly as possible and show strength of character in dealing with them. If he ignores problems or hopes that the situation will 'come right', he is opting out of one of the most important parts of his job. Some team managers reason that if the team is rewarded as a *whole* for winning, then the team should be disciplined as a *whole* for serious misconduct. Celtic, who had won the European Cup in 1967, fined its entire team a large sum of money for violence on the field while playing an over-aggressive South American club at a later date for the World Cup Championship in Argentina. This thinking is fraught with danger as its effects on team spirit could be disastrous for innocent players punished for offences committed by other players.

When the team manager decides to approach a player with a view to confronting and disciplining him, he might consider the following procedure to avoid possible conflict:

The reason

The team manager must think about why he has disciplinary action in mind and he must also be clear about the possible outcome of his action. Is the offence really so severe? At times team managers tend to over-react by confronting players when they are angry. It is always a good idea for the team manager to take time, before he confronts the player, to sit down and, keeping his emotions under control, plan coolly what he intends to say to the player.

The approach

The team manager must give some thought to the personality of the player and whether he is normally conscientious, or excitable, or lacks responsibility. When planning his approach, the team manager should reflect on what approaches have worked well with the player in the past. Does he normally react better to a quiet talk or to a more forceful approach? If a few approaches have failed with a particular player and he has blatantly and consistently flouted the rules, the team manager needs to try different approaches which may be based more on intuition than past experience and which require close monitoring of the player's subsequent reactions to them.

The environment

Thought needs to be given to where the team manager confronts the player. The training area or dressing-room or similar places are most familiar to the player, while the team manager's office is more alien territory. The team manager must not confront the player in front of his team-mates as the player can lose face and hold a grievance against the team manager for a long time to come. However, it is not always possible to avoid this as sometimes the player will seek confrontation with the team manager by breaking the rules in front of other players when the team manager is present. If the manager is psychologically strong he can let the player know what the limits are in terms of the player's conduct there and then; otherwise he can try to defuse the situation by telling the player to come to his office immediately where he can confront him on his own territory. The choice of place depends on the situation, but the office is usually more suitable for major offences and the training field, dressing-rooms, the club coach when travelling to and from matches, are usually better for more minor matters.

Summary:
Obviously, the need for discipline will vary from club to club but it is an important element in maintaining team spirit. There are several areas which are important to the building up and maintenance of team spirit,

but perhaps the most influential is the team manager/coach partnership. The team manager must try to make the difficult players accept that their conduct is causing a problem to the team. Then both can work together to improve the player's attitude. Team spirit is an irresistible force at its best but to maintain it requires determination, tact, courage and patience from the team manager and the coach.

9

INDIVIDUAL AND TEAM
PERFORMANCE ANALYSIS

In modern soccer, where success is very important, very little is left to chance at the higher levels of the game. Many coaches record and analyse the performance of their own players or team to try and find ways of increasing their effectiveness, and also that of teams they are due to meet in forthcoming matches, in order to detect weaknesses that can be exploited and strengths that require special attention. Analysis can be very valuable to the coach in team preparation and information can be gleaned from various sources – films, television, video, the 'live' competitive match (which is best), training sessions and the comments of his own players, who may have already played against the opposition.

The Analysis Model

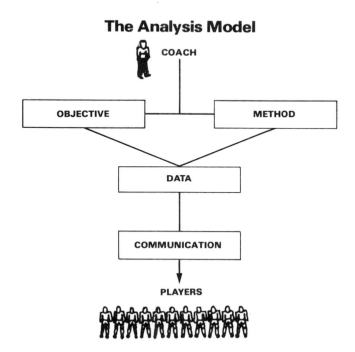

129

Objective

The coach must decide specifically *what* he wishes to analyse and *why* he is doing the analysis. Is it of an individual, a group, or the entire team? He may want to encourage a certain player to shoot more often at goal or to be more accurate with his passing; he may want to discover how players compare in terms of their running loads and work rate, or how effective the team's restarts have been during a match. The coach must be very clear at the outset about what he wishes to analyse and what benefits will accrue to the player(s) or team from the analysis.

Method

When he has decided on his objective(s) he must decide on the best method to use. A lot will depend on the quality of his assistants and how well they can record data, how detailed the analysis is to be, and the time available. Coaches who have access to sophisticated equipment (video, for example) can use it to analyse performance; however, good analysis is perfectly possible without expensive equipment.

Compiling data

The coach must compile the analysis from the collected data so that he can pass the results back to the player or team. For the exercise to be any use at all, the terms of reference must be clear; the analyst must know exactly what he is analysing and what constitutes a successful or unsuccessful count. For example, if a player's tackling is under scrutiny in a particular match, he may tackle an opponent, dispossessing him of the ball, only for another opponent to regain possession – would this be classified as a successful or an unsuccessful tackle?

Analysing the opposition

The modern game has become scientific. Teams now analyse the opposition to spot possible weaknesses which can be exploited and also strengths which the coach and players can plan to counteract. There are several reasons for scouting and analysing:

★ To gain any advantage over the opposition, technically, through skill, fitness or psychologically, all of which will help a team to win a match.
★ Knowing the opponent's strengths and weaknesses in advance can help in planning the strategy more effectively for the forthcoming match.
★ Psychologically, it can increase a team's confidence by giving it information about its opponents which lets the team feel that it has an advantage over the other team.

Sometimes, a coach does not scout or analyse the opposition because he feels that it is more important for his team to deal with its own approach and forget the opposition. Provided that the team is very strong, mature and experienced, this can be acceptable. More often,

130

however, no scouting or analysis takes place because of lack of time or lack of initiative — a feeling that is not worth the time and effort involved.

Scouting preparation

The coach may do the scouting himself or delegate it to an experienced, able assistant. The coach or scout should take the following steps:

★ Get a league fixture list so that the scouting schedule can be organised in advance.
★ Have a supply of scouting/analysis sheets prepared in advance.
★ Get to the ground early to ensure a good, comfortable spot with a good viewing position.

The recorder

To observe and record a match properly the recorder must try to find a spot where he can be relatively comfortable and free from distractions, for he will be required to concentrate hard for ninety minutes — longer for games which require extra time. This can be difficult, as many grounds do not have special facilities for match recorders, so it is wise to dress against the cold weather and make sure of a reasonably clear view of the pitch. A high position in the grandstand is good for seeing such things as systems or tactical aspects, while the coach is better off nearer ground level to observe individual players. To be objective the recorder must record what the player sees at ground level and not what the recorder can see at grandstand level. The recorder must be free from prejudices and chart the facts objectively, and if the coach is the recorder/analyst he must be completely honest in the analysis and be prepared to be proven wrong by the results of the analysis. Coaches and players alike are sure that their eyes never make mistakes and there is sometimes disagreement between them over match incidents! It is only human to try to prove yourself right and you may sub-consciously twist the facts and forget certain other incidents that occurred. The coach must not always rely on his memory; rather, he should try to collect factual evidence wherever possible.

Analysis methods

A creative coach can design many methods to chart and analyse players and teams' performances, but whatever method he uses should incorporate the following characteristics:

★ *Simplicity*
The analysis should be simple in design.
★ *Validity*
It should be accurate and keep to its terms of reference.
★ *Productivity*
The analysis must help player or team to improve their performance.

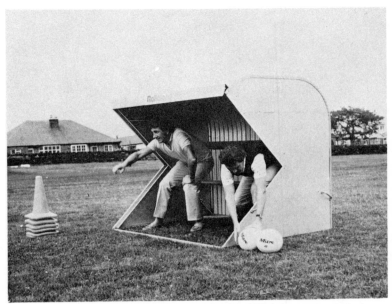

A successful partnership – Roy McFarland (left) and Mick Jones, respectively Team Manager and coach of newly-promoted Bradford City F.C.

★ *Efficiency*
The analysis should not involve the coach in the time-consuming chore of sorting through a mass of statistics – it should be as efficient and short as possible.

Analysis material

The following analysis sheets are samples of the type of material that I have used when analysing the performance of teams and players over the years. The analysis can be applied in three general areas:

Individual performance

Charting the individual's skill in technical, psychological or tactical performances. The individual player's success or failure rate of passing, shooting, covering in defence, goalkeeping, etc.

Team or group performance

Charting the opposition or own team's technical play. The system of play, restarts and goals scored or lost, etc.

Fitness performance

Charting players' physical output to see how hard they are working and what changes may need to be made in the training programme in terms of distance covered, number of sprints, jumps, etc.

Savile F.C.
Individual Performance Sheet

SUCCESS OBJECTIVE:	Player: J. Mellor Match: Thornton v. St. Bede's
	Date: Sat 5th Dec. Conditions: Fine, wet, heavy.

	Period		1st Half	T	2nd Half	T	Game	% Success
	Skills/Tactics						Total	
PLAYER PLAYS PASS TO A TEAMMATE WHO MUST HAVE REASONABLE CHANCE OF CONTROLLING BALL.	PASSING	S	|||||||	6	||||||	7	13	
		U	xxxxxxxx	9	xxxxxx	6	15	46%
		T		15		13	28	
PLAYER RETAINS POSSESSION FROM A PASS OR CLEARANCE AND ALLOWS HIM TO PASS, SHOOT OR DRIBBLE.	CONTROL	S						
		U						
		T						
PLAYER HEADS BALL ON GOAL TARGET OR TO TEAMMATE TO GIVE HIM CHANCE OF POSSESSION	HEADING	S						
		U						
		T						
PLAYER TACKLES TO RETAIN BALL, PLAY IT OUT OF PLAY OR TO A TEAMMATE WHO KEEPS POSSESSION	TACKLING	S						
		U						
		T						
PLAYER DRIBBLES BALL PAST A DEFENDER AND RETAINS FULL POSSESSION	DRIBBLING	S						
		U						
		T						
PLAYER HITS BALL ON GOAL TARGET TO SCORE, FORCE GOAL KICK OR DEFENDER TO SAVE IT.	SHOOTING	S						
		U						
		T						

SUMMARY: This analysis was done on a schoolboy player aged 14 years, who played centreback and Captain and gave a strong performance in a team which was beaten 1-5. Many of the passes were give under reasonable pressure and on a bumpy pitch to two target men who were often outnumbered and heavily marked. All this made accuracy more difficult. However, on the positive side, the players passes were all in a forward direction and attempted to penetrate. All the passes were given with the right foot even when it was easier to play the ball with the left foot. His basic range of passing techniques was quite good but his timing and pace of pass needs working on. He tended to run with the ball at times and passed the ball on the run when he could have composed himself first before passing.

Huddersfield Town v Team F.C.

DATE: Saturday, 17th October, 1981   **Result**
VENUE: Leeds Road, Huddersfield.   **1 – 1**
CONDITIONS: Cold, damp. Pitch heavy and
                      muddy.

Pattern of Play

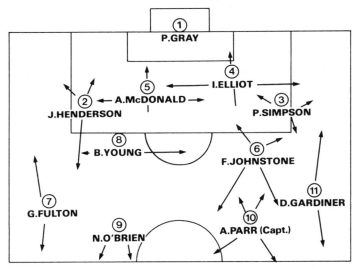

⑫ R. POOLE.

TEAM F.C. Began match as above in a 4-4-2 formation
with two withdrawn wingers. After the injury to Elliot ④ they
reorganised by using Gardiner ⑪ as sweeper and drafting
in Poole ⑫ to fill in for Gardiner in a similar role.
As the game progressed Fulton was pushed into a more
advanced wingers position.

The match analysis is one that I did for a League Club. To maintain the players'/team's confidentiality, the dates and names have been changed.

Individual Players

No.	Name	Hgt.	Details
1.	P.GRAY	6.1	Bulky, top heavy physique which made mobility off his line and getting to crosses difficult. Excellent right foot kicker of the ball. Overall a casual approach to the job.
2.	J.HENDERSON	5.5	Sturdy and experienced player who is one of the 'Playmakers' of the team. Calm under pressure and uses ball well and is suprisingly fast for his age. Gets forward well.
3.	P.SIMPSON	6.2	Tall gangly lad who plays with serious limitations and seems to lack confidence when ball is on his left foot and where opponents dribble at him with the ball.
4.	I.ELLIOT	5.11	Tends to play a little deeper than his other centre back - went off after 15 mins with injury and due to the time factor he could not be realistically assessed.
5.	A.McDONALD	5.10	Bearded, compact centre back who gets on with the job without looking especially commanding on the ground or in the air. Did not like to move to flanks.
6.	F.JOHNSTONE	5.10	An athletic lad who was full of running worked hard in defence and especially in attack to get up and support his front men. an 'educated' left foot.
7.	G.FULTON	5.9	A young inexperienced player who is very quick with ball at his feet if given the chance. lacks the know-how to make space to turn with the ball. Defends well.
8.	B.YOUNG	5.7	More of an 'anchor-man' who works quietly to fill important space central to right side. Is not very creative and does not get forward much.
9.	N.O'BRIEN	5.9	A young goalscoring 'star' who looked lethargic and uninvolved for long periods but came alive in the penalty area where he was very quick and dangerous. Scored one goal.
10.	A.PARR	5.6	Played the captains part with his non-stop running and 'battling' up front. Played more as a target man and has good control, mobility and 'linking' skills. Good partner with OBrien
11.	D.GARDINER	5.9	Started in left midfield role to stop the over-lap running of the Huddersfield F.C. right full back but later reverted to 'sweeper' role. Good left foot and economical player.
12.	R.POOLE	5.10	Came on and played as deep winger and did well. Powerful runner and good utility player who did his defensive and attacking duties well.

Restarts

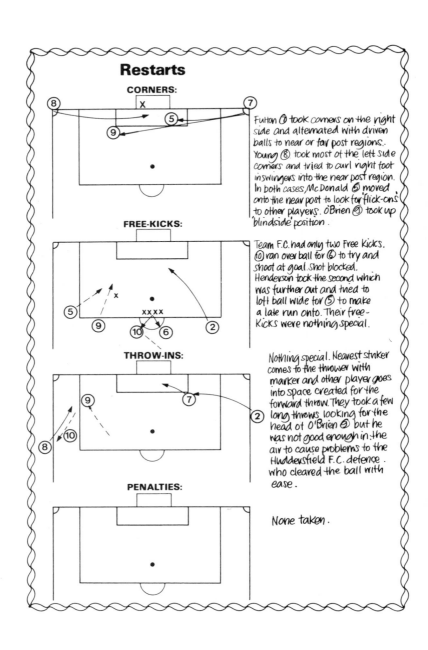

CORNERS:

Fulton ⑦ took corners on the right side and alternated with driven balls to near or far post regions. Young ⑧ took most of the left side corners and tried to curl right foot inswingers into the near post region. In both cases, McDonald ⑤ moved onto the near post to look for flick-ons to other players. O'Brien ⑨ took up 'blindside' position.

FREE-KICKS:

Team F.C. had only two free kicks. ⑩ ran over ball for ⑥ to try and shoot at goal. Shot blocked. Henderson took the second which was further out and tried to loft ball wide for ⑤ to make a late run onto. Their free-kicks were nothing special.

THROW-INS:

Nothing special. Nearest striker comes to the thrower with marker and other player goes into space created for the forward throw. They took a few long throws looking for the head of O'Brien ⑨ but he was not good enough in the air to cause problems to the Huddersfield F.C. defence who cleared the ball with ease.

PENALTIES:

None taken.

Summary

Huddersfield F.C. dominated the match for long periods and threatened to over-run team F.C. who managed to hang on to secure draw which was rather fortunate. Their basic style is to 'pack' midfield and keep things tight at the back and look for chances to break and counter-attack at speed. They are quite well organised but I feel they give the initiative too much to the opposition by stifling their main attackers into containing, rather than attacking roles where they look quite dangerous on the few times they broke.

IN ATTACK:

They play mostly through their two most experienced players, Henderson ② and Parr ⑩ who seem to spark off most play. The team channel much of the play through these two and set off from there. The Huddersfield centre backs got tight on Parr to stop his supply and to prevent him from turning with the ball but they did not have so much success with Henderson who started a lot of attacking moves from deep, and sometimes, advanced, positions. They play on a fairly wide front with the wingers potentially dangerous, especially Fulton ⑦ who is very quick and direct. They are good at lulling teams into a false sense of security before breaking out with Johnstone ⑥ making long runs and O'Brien ⑨ sneaking in behind the defence when possible.

IN DEFENCE:

Huddersfield F.C. caused their 'Back-Four' problems by a lot of good runs and movement in the final attacking third of the pitch. The centre backs lacked speed and mobility to some extent and did not like to come out wide from central positions for fear of being exposed. The goalkeeper and back four are not particularly big and Huddersfield F.C. gave them a few problems with crosses, especially at restarts where they were lucky not to lose a few more goals. Team F.C. use up the ability of men in front of the left back Simpson ③ to cover and shield him. He could be exploited if he could be isolated. Overall, Team F.C. are a fairly well-balanced team but can be exploited along the lines given.

SIGNED *Malcolm Cook* DATE 17/10/81

Savile F.C.
Team Performance Sheet

SUCCESS OBJECTIVE:

Venue:_____ Match:_____ v._____

Date:_____ Conditions:_____

	Period		1st Half				2nd Half				Game	
	Time /mins.		15	30	45	▼	60	75	90	▼	▼	%
	Skills/Tactics					T				T	Total	Success
ON TARGET TO SCORE OR FORCE A SAVE.	SHOTS:	S										
		U										
		T										
ATTACK: AT GOAL OR TO KEEP POSSESSION OF BALL DEFEND: TO WIN BALL AND CLEAR FROM DANGER ZONE.	HEADERS:	S										
		U										
		T										
ENDING WITH BALL POSSESSION WITHIN 2/3 PASSES	THROW-INS:	S										
		U										
		T										
ENDING WITH SHOT OR HEADER ATTEMPT AT GOAL.	FREE KICKS:	S										
		U										
		T										
ENDING WITH SHOT OR HEADER ATTEMPT AT GOAL.	CORNERS:	S										
		U										
		T										
No. OF TIMES ADJUDGED TO BE OFFSIDE (WHICH PLAYERS)	OFF-SIDES:	S										
		U										
		T										

SUMMARY:

Savile F.C.
Individual Fitness Performance Sheet

Success Criteria:		Match: _____ v _____ Date: _____
		Conditions: _____

	Period ➡	1st Half				2nd Half				Game
	Time mins.	15	30	45	T	60	75	90	T	T
	Skills/Tactics									
Flat-out dash	SPRINTS:									
Less than flat out runs	CRUISING:									
Runs in backward direction	BACKWARDS:									
No. of jumps	JUMPS:									
Either direction	TURNS:									
SUMMARY:										

Advantages and disadvantages

The performance analysis can be effective if used properly. The coach should know and understand the major advantages and disadvantages:

ADVANTAGES

1. *Motivational*
Can motivate players by showing their strengths in comparison with others or by identifying weaknesses on which the player can work.

2. *Aids communication*
Provides the coach with good opportunities to communicate with the players. The player can be shown clearly on which areas he should focus his attention in order to improve.

3. *Reinforcement*
Evidence from the analysis can be used to reinforce the coach's case when confronting a stubborn and unrealistic player who refuses to accept his weaknesses or do anything about them. However, the coach needs to be careful when using the analysis for this purpose as it can alienate a stubborn player.

DISADVANTAGES

1. *De-motivational*
Often players feel that their play is being put under the microscope, which could mean that they will be dropped if they do not perform satisfactorily. Consequently they feel threatened and mistrust the analysis because they think it is intended to show up their weaknesses.

2. *Endangers credibility*
The players can lose faith in the match analysis if it records their performances falsely or inaccurately; hence the coach will lose credibility.

3. *Time-consuming*
It often takes a long time to record, assess and analyse the data correctly and the recorders may need to be trained to do the match analysis.

Summary:
The player and team performance analysis can be a valuable tool for the coach if used properly. It can help him to spot what is going wrong with his players and team and motivate them to improve their effectiveness. It can also help his team to win matches by locating strengths and weaknesses in the opposition that require special attention by his team.

Using this data

When giving the results of the analysis to the players, the coach must ensure that all the possible reasons for the final counts have been taken into consideration before presenting the facts to the team. For example, the analysis may show that a team's front strikers did not get many shots in. However, the team may have been under pressure by the opposition for long periods and as a result the strikers did not receive much service. The coach must remember that the performance/match analysis is only a *guide* which he can check to see if any regular patterns emerge. For example, a coach should try to record details of how all the goals for and against his team were made, over the entire season. He may discover that a large proportion of goals given away were headed, indicating that his defence is poor at dealing with balls crossed in from the flanks. For the following season he may decide to try to acquire one or more central defenders or a goalkeeper who can deal with this type of ball, or he may give his existing defenders and goalkeeper concentrated practice on crosses, and generally make his defence aware of the danger and the need to improve this aspect of play.

The coach must sort out the data and present it in a form his players can understand. When I was coach at Bradford City A.F.C. I did many match analyses for Manager George Mulhall on the teams that the club was due to meet, giving him a detailed and comprehensive analysis, showing him the key factors at a glance. As we could identify certain trends, he could make the need for change or increased practice apparent to the players. Psychologically, it is better if the coach can present the analysis at the *match inquest* a day or two after the match or a few days before the next one as it will have more impact this way. The players should learn from their mistakes while the game is still fresh in their minds; equally, they should feel prepared for the forthcoming match and be aware of any surprises that the opposition may try to spring on them. When preparing to meet a specific team or opponent, coaches must be careful not to over-emphasise their strengths; players will tend to become uneasy and anxious if they hear too much about the good points of their opponents. Conversely, players can become complacent if too much emphasis is laid on the various weak points of the opposition. The information should be presented in a matter-of-fact manner that conveys to the players that provided each person plays to the agreed match-plan, they have a more than reasonable chance of winning.